When the Veil Drops

By Samara Alexander

ISBN-13: 9781451541939
ISBN-10: 1451541937

Dedication

⌒〜⌒

I am dedicating this book to my mother, *Haja* (honorary title for people who made the pilgrimage) Fatima.

Mom, I want you to know that you have done everything humanly possible to make me a devout Muslim. You raised me well. You put me in memorizing Koran classes so my heart would have eternal light. I won memorizing Koran competitions for you. You stood by me when I refused arranged marriage proposals. You did not fail me in any way.

I know that you pray every day for my guidance. I know that you devote all of your fasting in Ramadan to pray for my sins to be forgiven. I know that you volunteer to fast every Monday and Thursday to pray for me. I know that you wake up every night for three hours to read Koran and pray for me. I have heard you. I know that you believe in Qadr/destiny and that everything is maktoob/written.

Mom, I wrote my own destiny. I live my own life and I love you.

Samara

Disclaimer

I believe that any writing should be considered pornographic only if it intends to be pornographic. My objective is not to arouse readers. The pornographic nature of my writing is a byproduct of writing about dating.

I practice my first amendment right of free speech. I use the word "pussy"; if that offends you, please do not buy this book. I am not going to use beaver, Kurt Vonnegut's expression in *Breakfast of Champions*. I will not use a euphemism of a furry animal with a flat tail. To use beaver would mean that I am lacking a penis. I have a beautiful "Pussy."

Names have been changed except when I did not feel like it. I have not slept with any politician yet so who cares if indoor Mark is in fact a Mark.

Contents

Part One

Part Two
⟳

Part Three
⟳

Acknowledgments

A special thank you goes to my friend Anastasia. She is an amazing artist who contributed the sketche of the zipped mouth.

A special thank you goes to my former student Jeremy. He is an astute person whose advise has changed my life.

A special thank you to my ex husband, who took my virginity and opened the can of sexual worms. Divorce was his idea and I thank him. He was gracious enough to divorce me, which allowed me to experience the joy of sex.

A special thank you to my neighbors, a married couple, who are my constant reminders that marriage should be only temporary. Most of the time, after hearing their fights, I want to petition for their divorce myself.

A special thank you to Carolyn, my publisher friend, for her sound pieces of advice. One day she said, "Sam, that book has no legs!" While I was not sure if that was an American expression or just editor talk, I knew that I needed to install wheels and run with it. She encouraged me to do this second edition.

A special thank you to my editor, Jami; her work on my second book encouraged me to do a new edition of the first one. I thank her for suffering through my "Arabized" English and keeping my voice.

A special thank you to my best friend Steve. I met him in 1997 and he was one of my first American friends. His emotional support all these years means a lot to me. I thank him for being the best girlfriend a woman can have.

A special thank you goes to Cyrus Webb for all his encouragement and support. Cyrus invited me to speak on his Conversations live blog talk radio and connected me to other radio hosts. Cyrus is a rare gem.

The second edition:

The second edition includes all the stories from the first edition and one new story. I have added a part two, which includes short essays on Islam, on wearing the veil, on homosexuality, on marriage, on erotic excitement, and concluding remarks. Part three includes more poems.

When I wrote the first edition, I just wrote my story. I did not place it within the proper context. I did not explain the archetypal images that I grew up with or the cultural conditioning of my background. I found out that it was hard for some readers to see beyond the stories.

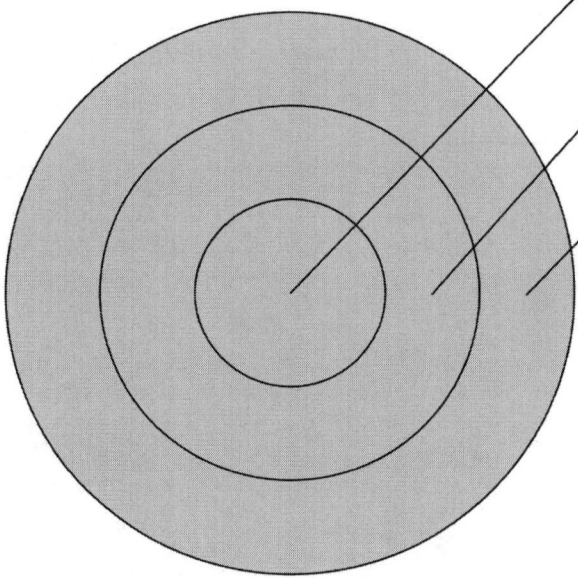

My story

Family
cluster

Cultural
influences

Introduction

I came to the United States at the age of twenty-three, still wearing my invisible Muslim chastity belt. I did not receive any sexual education. I was a virgin who believed that sex was a long hug. A woman got pregnant if people were naked.

At the airport before I left my native country, one of my married young aunts felt courageous. She yelled my very first sexual advice. She said, "No matter how painful it is, let him do it." On the long flight over, I threw up for hours. I am sure that she meant to comfort me. However, she scared the hell out of me.

I grew up without any dating experience. To be divorced and start dating was similar to doing field experience in a world that I did not understand. Sure, I used the regular girlfriends/ informants, but I needed to have my first-hand experience. In my field work, I used an accidental sampling technique. I did not use a purposive sampling and target specific types of men. Additionally, I did not want to seek participants on the extreme — just regular guys.

The delimitation of my study:

First, I did not go black. My girlfriends scared me with the "Do not come back" clause.

Second, torture in sex and water works are not part of my taste, therefore they are beyond the scope of this study

My family cluster:

I absorbed a dehumanizing attitude from my father. He transferred that beast to me. I feel it lurking inside. I shield all my loved ones from it. The Arabic cultural conditioning taught me rigid gender roles. I loved how my father never had to get his own cup of water. He would ask my mother. Sometimes he would just motion with his hand and she jumped to get his water. I like how she pampered him. For me, the husband deserves to have his feet washed and his back rubbed daily.

But I did not like how my father did not appreciate it. What hurts me the most is that my mother still accepts daily verbal abuse from him. I resent my mother's inability to shut my father up. The older my father gets the more abusive he gets. He is older than my mother by about fifteen years, which is normal in the Arabic culture.

When my mother came to visit, I took her to therapy session for her depression and I had to be present to translate her words into English. We had to lie every time because she couldn't let my father know about it. After the fifth session, he accidentally learned about it after a nurse called us to reschedule. He forbade her to go. She convinced me that it was her decision. "Yes, I am depressed but I would never kill myself. Suicide is against Islam. However, I can't disobey my husband; that is a sin," she said. I failed to explain to my mother the concept of quality of life. When I called to cancel the sessions with the counselor, she was relieved. She said that although she accepted the sessions, she thought that these sessions were more damaging to me than helpful to my mother.

I came from a line of strong women, even if that strength took a resilient passive form in my mother's case. I identified with my grandmother who was a character larger than life. She stood against my father and saved me from circumcision and few arranged marriages. She was the exception to all the Arab female victims that I continually see around me. She belonged to the early feminists. She fell in love with my grandfather, while my mother did not get to see my father before their engagement.

My grandmother wanted to name me Huda for Huda Shaarawi, an iconic Egyptian feminist. My grandmother must have told me the story of how Huda took off her head covering in a train station and saved thousands of women from wearing head coverings. I share the same birthday with that female activist. My grandmother thought that was a good omen, but my father disregarded her request to name me Huda.

My great-grandmother *Haja* Khadija died when I was nine-years-old. I wish that I had more time with her. She was a successful business woman who owned the apartment building where she lived. She did not allow people to call her by her name. She was called Mama el Haja. *Haja* is a title you receive after making the holy pilgrimage to Mecca. She was a two-time widow. We talked about her two marriages. Both husbands died at very early ages. Her first husband died after three years of marriage and my great-grandfather died after five years of marriage. She took me in her room one day and told me a secret: "Divorce was frowned upon; but that's why men had to die."

Cultural conditioning:

It has been over a year since the first edition of the book and I am still answering the same question about what possessed me to write a book about sex. With the sales record of the first edition, let's all agree the reason could be neither fame nor fortune. The reason I wrote my book is my belief that equality between the sexes starts from sexual freedom. Sexuality is tied to reproduction in the Arab, world which perpetuates the need to control women.

A typical Arab male is an unevolved primate who feels the need to subjugate the female to his will. I am not saying all Arab men, of course; there are some who are slowly evolving. I have met "Progressive Arab Americans," but they are only willing to accept their wives contributing their income to the household. They still retain the right to control everything. They never offer to help at the house while they enjoy the additional income of their overworked wives.

I grew up learning that I was never going to play the main role in my own life movie. I could only play the supporting actress role. It was only through the satisfaction and total obedience to my husband that I could receive the best supporting actress award from God. I had to refuse that role assigned by culture. I had to read and connect myself with the strong feminists in my history.

It is not in a male dominated culture's best interest to document those wonderful examples of self-determined women. Instead of showing strong examples and celebrating the achievement of women, the culture perpetuated the myth of co-dependency. I grew up hearing that "the shadow of a man is better than the shadow of a wall." That meant that being with a man — any man — is better than being alone. I look at some examples of married women and I tell you honestly, I prefer my wall. Another common saying is "a girl has a broken wing."

There are several archetypal images which represent the simplistic reductive generalization of Arab female characters:

Amina and Zanouba: These two women were characters in stories written by Naguib Mahfouz, an Egyptian writer and Nobel prize winner. Amina was the wife who obeyed. She fed the children after the father ate. She did not go anywhere without her husband's permission, as prescribed by Islam. The day she went to go to the mosque without permission, she twisted her ankle and felt it was a punishment from God.

Zanouba was a singer; the writer called her the night lady. She was the mistress of Amina's husband. As a child growing up, I wanted to be Amina and Zanouba to my husband.

Scheherazade: She is by far the most famous character in Middle Eastern history. She was married to King Shahryar, who married and killed a virgin every night. The tale goes that she conquered her husband's mind by telling him a thousand and one stories for a thousand and one nights. I can't accept that she conquered the mind without sex. I believe the tradition removed that part. In one of my poems, I made Scheherazade a sexually frustrated woman. I recorded it on YouTube and it had a large number of viewers.

I feel the need to share a few examples of female writers whose writings encouraged me as a child. I often wonder how many of women's struggles went unrecorded. Future generations of girls need a new tradition where women are celebrated. There are several examples of strong women. I am sharing some examples of strong-willed women. Early generations left enough bread crumbs and we just need to follow them home.

Iqabal Baraka: She is a talented and courageous Egyptian writer who wrote about early feminists. She also holds inspiring views against the veil. I recommend reading all her books.

Nawal El Sadawi: I recommend reading all her books. She is a pioneer who championed the cause against female circumcision, the mutilation and a crime against humanity. The surgery is done for the sole purpose of not allowing women to feel pleasure during intercourse. It is originally an African practice, and while it is said that circumcision and clitoridectomy are not part of Islamic teaching, why do so many Muslims practice it? It is not even enough to ban it, because it would continue in a clandestine way. To make illegal would only mean that doctors would refuse to do it, for fear of losing their licenses. Then families would seek nurses or even barbers using unclean tools. That would eventually make it worse.

The only solution is to change the culture that condones it. We need to educate people and raise the level of consciousness about the dangers of such practices. Nawal El Sadawi also exposed some incest cases in Egypt. One day, I was watching a television interview with her. I was so happy. I yelled at the TV set; "Amen, sister; let's change that shared belief system and affect social change."

My mother heard me from the kitchen, came to the living room, and turned off the television. She said, "Nawal is ugly and only ugly women can afford to be defiant because men do not want them anyway."

My mother is a prime example of the subordinate who imitates, assimilates, and adopts the dominant's values. I feel sorry for my mother who was always trying to save me from my own crazy ideas. I said, "Then call me ugly because I swear by God, I will be defiant."

Now that you have read the longest introduction, you are ready to read about how a girl born with a broken wing, soared so high …

Part One

〜

There, in this risky enterprise, dense with the fullness of parts of human sexuality and its informing spirit, we will find our true identity.
Ann and Barry Ulanov, *Transforming Sexuality*

Sharmoota

People say that what they are all seeking is a meaning of life. I don't think that's what we are really seeking. I think that what we are seeking is an experience of being alive.

Joseph Campbell, *The Power of Myth*

The word whore in Arabic is *sharmoota*. It literally means rag, because a whore is like a rag where men wipe their filth. I was six-years-old when my mother explained to me that *sharmoota* is a woman who had sex with more than one man. I asked her if she meant more than one man at the same time. My question was deemed insolent. It earned me my first slap on the face. My question was out of ignorance. However my mother's reaction made me wonder.

We teach our daughters to share their toys except for one: the husband. Well, that is the only toy that needs to be shared. There is an old Arab saying; it goes like this: "Those who dance on the stairs no one sees them nor hears them." I always felt that I was dancing on the stairs between my two cultures, and in my dance I learned that there is no cheating proof husband. Polygamy is about the only concept in Islam that makes sense. I understand Western women do not like to share their husbands. Nevertheless, they do end up sharing just part-time. The mistress enjoys a lot of benefits but has no rights. Imagine your husband feels lust toward another woman, then he has to come and ask for permission to propose to her. Men have to commit twice so they think long and hard before they do it.

If your man can have an erection, he can have an affair. I hold this opinion to be the first axiom of life. The good news is that if he comes back, then he loves you and all that Jazz. Or it might just be the mortgage, but at least he comes back. A man presented with an open pussy opportunity and declines is simply not a keeper.

1

You need to dust him off and put him out half price at your next garage sale.

Dr. Bickerford pushed my harem button. My guess is that I came equipped with it. I just did not know it existed. I did not want to have an affair. I was a *sharmoota*, whore by Arabic standards, since I was touched by more than one man. Sleeping with a married man would make a *sharmoota* by American standards. I simply did not want to be an American *sharmoota*. With that said, let me tell you how I found myself knee deep in an affair.

I was in Dr. Bickerford's office. Somehow as we were discussing my pituitary gland disorder which was causing me to have day dreams, he lifted my fuchsia-colored dress and fucked me in his office. I did not expect him to fuck me. It was a surprise fuck. It all happened so quickly and I became the star of the first silent porn movie. Nurses were out there. We could have been interrupted. I wondered if they would join us. He did have that large-breasted blond nurse. I was living one of my daydreams. I was not attracted to my doctor, but the fact that he took charge and dominated me made him the only one for me.

Two days after our first encounter, and yes, I call it an encounter as I would describe it as a mythical, epic, out-of-this-world experience, he called me into his office to apologize. I did not recognize his face covered with all that dreadful regret. He explained that he had been a happily married man for nine years. He repeated that he loved his wife and that he had never cheated on her. I later found out that is the standard line given by cheating husbands. A cheating husband will tell you anything to justify his guilt. I was bored. I started to have an inner dialogue, slightly more interesting. I wondered if I should start calling him Robert. I believe fucking guarantees a first name basis. I could not understand why he was talking to me about his faithfulness or unfaithfulness. I was not his priest. I was his sin.

He talked and talked and I decided that it was time for me to dominate. I went down on my knees and I sucked his cock. His juice was my lunch. I refused to eat dinner that day. I wanted to keep the taste of Robert as long as I could.

Two days after my second visit, I called his office and asked for him to refill my prescription. The nurse could not find the name

2

of the medicine in my file so she gave him the message. He called me back and asked for my address. Twenty minutes later he called to say that he could not make it. I could hear his voice. I did not answer. I walked to my door. He was standing there with tears in his eyes. I kissed his eyes and tasted his tears.

We had our first triathlon. He started with an open ocean swim, then hopped on and cycled; the final leg of the competition was a twenty minute marathon. We fucked on the floor with the door still open. As he was getting dressed he told me that this could never happen again. He said that God was watching him. I laughed. I told him that God is not a pervert and chances are that he would not watch porn for three hours. Finally, I got him to laugh. As he walked out my door, he said that was the last time. I reached out and grabbed his dick, which was curiously still hard. Maybe it was not, but it responded to my gentle goodbye touch.

The next day, I called his cell and left a message that I was naked in bed and that the key to my apartment was under the mat. Of course he came over. That day I introduced him to my other partner, Sean, the dildo. I had to name my dildo. It is more personal that way.

I said: "Robert, I would like you to meet Sean."

He asked why Sean.

I said, "Sean for Sean Connery, of course." I told him that I wanted to feel like his slut. He laughed. He was intrigued and asked what I had in mind. I said that it was my day to have Sean and Robert at the same time. Sean got the front and Robert took the back. My childhood question was answered. Indeed a woman can have two penises at the same time. I came close — a penis and a dildo — which felt good!

Arabs believe that if you kiss someone on the eye, you will be separated. I kissed Robert's eyes and we ended up separating. Affairs should not be planned. It is just too boring. Plan a vacation, a party, or retirement, but do not plan an affair. My affair with Robert lasted two months. He started the affair. He ended the affair. He called it his temporary insanity. I enjoyed it. The affair reconciled my two cultures. I became *sharmoota* by all standards.

The proposal

What is manliness, anyway? The fact that we have to ask suggests that something has gone awry in the garden.

Kathleen Parker, *Save the males*

"You are the one for me," said Jason.

No, we were not in bed, so I could not forgive him for saying that. I had to leave Jason. I had to leave Jason because he believed it. A woman has the ability to feel that a man is the one. A man should never feel that a woman is the one. For me, that is a man who thinks with his estrogen. Think about it: the woman is the body of the car and the man is the engine. A car without the engine is just junk, but an engine without a body is still an engine.

Women are interchangeable, but men are not. I hold this sentence to be the second axiom of life. There are only two things which separate women from another one: First, her sexual skills, which can be taught, and second, her willingness to do unspeakable things for her man. The one thing that separates a man from another one is the prized cucumber and that, my friend, is an innate talent. A man can compensate or be a pleaser. The only things that matter are size, length, and width. If you come well-equipped, you can always learn how to hit better. Practice makes a perfect performer. However, you just can't show up to a baseball game with a table tennis racket.

Arab men figured it out. If a woman has the experience of more than one man, she would know when she has been short-changed. It took me a while to understand why Muslim men prefer their women in the same way they like their olive oil — extra virgin. They could not deal with competition. They had to eliminate it.

Western women figured this out as well. If a man fucks more than one woman, he will find out that he can satisfy or even be

5

more satisfied with another woman. Western women could not deal with competition. They had to eliminate it.

Here is my attempt at a sound argument of the day: I have heard a feminist say that the Koran was written by a man because of polygamy. If that premise were true then the Bible was definitely written by a woman because of monogamy. Marriage was the ploy to give good men a life sentence. Men started to wise up about the whole marriage ploy. Western women are no fools. They had a backup plan: Romance. It is the second trick to get any man believing that what he has with his woman is unique. Well, it is not.

Jason fit my personal profile for a lover. He was American with Nordic features. He was six feet two inches tall with blue eyes. He had the 007 job. He looked like Pierce Brosnan so he definitely replaced my Sean Connery fantasy. He spoke Arabic fluently. He called me sharmoota in bed, which drove me over the edge. He loved being pampered by his Arab woman. I washed his feet when he came home from work. I gave him a massage every night. Like a good Muslim woman, I initiated sex twice a day. He loved it when I kissed his ass.

Why did he have to ruin everything and propose to me? Why couldn't he act strong? Why couldn't he dump me once or twice and make me compete for him? He was the product of American pop culture. I blame the Power Puff girls! While empowering women, we emasculated the men. Have you ever watched *Johnny Test?* It is a current cartoon about a silly boy and his two genius sisters. The media went from the Barbie twins to the genius twins. His father stays home cooking meatloaf and cleaning while his mother is a successful real estate agent. The media went from telling women, "You do not need a man to be strong," to saying, "Men, are they really necessary?" If we do not change the image of men for young growing boys, we will witness the end of Man. It is time to have another John Wayne. Maybe I exaggerate. Arabs normally do, but that is how I feel about it.

When Jason proposed to me, he pulled a Mel Gibson in *What Women Want.* You know which scene: Mel Gibson asked Helen Hunt to rescue him. My American girlfriends could not understand why I left Jason. One female friend actually asked me if the ring was small. Well, it was not. Nothing that Jason offered was small.

American women who had him before me had him castrated. Of course, I adore the penis but I can't love a man without the balls. He cried over the breakup. He sent me messages for a year. His behavior confirmed that I made the right decision. Jason worshipped me. I could not be with a man whom I viewed as weak, even if I was his weakness.

A true 007 man gets a new woman in every movie. No matter how great it felt between us that could not be duplicated. I may have large boobs and a sweet pussy, but I will not take part of the woman's scam. A woman, any woman, can be replaced.

Jack M.D.

It is the imperfections of life that are lovable.
Joseph Campbell, *The Power of Myth*

I successfully landed my first blowjob eight years ago. I was naïve and thirty-years-old with no female friends. Jack gave me the honor of sucking his dick. Each job lasted an hour to two hours. I am a perfectionist by nature and I believe in education. Naturally I started to watch porn to perfect my technique. I prefer to watch porn on mute and I watched a lot of it. I turned to Jenna Jameson for inspiration. She did deliver. Sucking Jack replaced prayers for me. It was my new commitment. Jack allowed a novice to suck his dick, but by the end he had a pro. Let me tell you how it all started with Jack M.D.

If any man deserves the M.D. initials after his name, it would be Jack. Before you start thinking that my protagonist heals people, let me explain how I use it. For me, M.D. represents masturbation dependent. In Arabic, the expression to jack off is "hit the ten." I have no idea why they need to use the ten fingers. That practice is called the "Secret Habit." It is forbidden by religion. In fact, "*Nick Nafesk*" is an insult in Arabic and it literally means "fuck yourself." It is very demeaning because you could not find a man, a woman, even a goat, and you are fucking yourself.

On a Wednesday six years ago, I had lunch with my friend Jack. He asked about cursing in Arabic, and I explained the expression. He laughed and said that he did just that twice a day. I was intrigued as I had not seen that before. My inner slut asked him if I could watch him and maybe give him a hand. Jack said, "If I show you mine, would you show me yours?" It seemed like a fair transaction. I was ready for my first show-and-tell until Jack said that he was not circumcised. A ringing screamed in my head — a gentile — and I was saved by this bell. I said that I needed to get back to my office and left.

It took Jack two weeks of lunches and surprise gifts to reopen the discussion again. He showed me an article about circumcised and uncircumcised men. For two weeks, my Arabic sexual ignorance gave me nightmares and horror scenarios. Then I decided it was just a penis. How bad could it be? He explained that the foreskin retracts with an erection. He made it sound like when the show starts the curtain lifts up. In my Arabic mind, I finally understood: it is a penis with a veiled face. We went to my home. I showed him and he showed me. I was a little disappointed. He was aroused and the veil dropped.

I joined Jdate website. I was a Muslim, but my men of choice were Jews. A little unorthodox, I know. There were financially successful and definitely circumcised. However none of them could take a Muslim girl home to mommy. I cooked lunch and invited my friend Jack to tell him about my failed Jewish conquest. He talked about his failed marriage and how his wife cheated on him. I was on a desperate road in Horny Ville when I slept with him.

As the relationship progressed, I slowly found out that Jack was an M.D. Between my mouth and my boobs, he had all he needed. I asked him about my belly dancing strong muscles. Nothing could compete with his strong hands. I still initiated sex. Jack allowed me to ride. As long as he did not have to do anything, he was okay with having sex.

I loved Jack and his "It is all about me" attitude. My relationship with Jack is the longest relationship in my life. I do not really know why it lasted as long as it did. The relationship presented years of sexual frustration and obedience to an ungrateful man. If I never have to see his wrinkled sac of shrunk balls, it will be too soon.

Although we broke up a year-and-a-half ago, at 10:30 or 10:45 p.m. every night Jack still calls me or sends me a text. The message will vary from saying goodnight or asking a question about my happiness. I do not answer his calls or read his messages. However, I know that his messages mean one thing: "I just jacked off and I thought about your boobs." I look at my silenced phone and smile. I look at men differently now. If a man gives me a strong handshake, I cross him off from my "to do" list. Strong hands are what I now call competition.

De La Chambre

"The said Man-Mountain shall confine his walks to our principal high roads, and not offer to walk or lie down in a meadow or field of corn."
Jonathan Swift, *Gulliver's Travels*

To fuck Richard or not to fuck Richard, that was my question. I was on the horns of a dilemma. I had a crush on Richard De La Chambre for nine years. In his California size bed. I had to confront my necessary truth: either direction I chose, the consequences would be dire. If I chose to fuck him, I could get addicted to his gargantuan sized penis. If I chose not to fuck him, I would live the rest of my life wondering.

Let me rewind the tape and tell you about how I met Richard De La Chambre in 2001. I had an address, a name, and a job interview. I was lost. I was nervous and worried. He stopped to help. Richard is 6 foot 4, right at the limit of my acceptable height for a man. I felt safe and secure. He escorted me to my destination. I felt that his dick had a presence. It was there looking at me through his pants. I got high picturing his dick. I entered my job interview confident and happy. I impressed everyone and got the job.

Our paths crossed again in 2002. This time I met him at a work function. He asked if he could bring me a drink. I declined. He apologized and said, "Ah, the Muslim thing." People drink to lower their inhibitions. If he knew me, he would have known that I have no inhibition. Someone came to talk to him. I walked away.

I met him again in 2004. I told my friend Sarah that I had a crush on Richard De La Chambre. She said that since I only had two sexual partners, I was not the right match for the wild and legendary Richard. He was single, in his late forties. His reputation as a player was scary to Sarah, but I knew that he was my kind of man. Nevertheless, I took Sarah's advice and kept my distance.

Two years ago, Richard transferred back into town. I saw him in the hallway. I stopped him. I gathered up all my courage and said to him, "You have been on the top of my to-do list for years now." Richard turned red. He took my email address and we started to talk. I started to call him king. He loved my eyes, so he started to call me Nefert.

One day, he complained about neck pain. Since I was a masseuse by hobby, I offered him a massage. He invited me over. I went to his place on a recon mission. I was so excited that I was finally going to see Richard De La Chambre naked. He did not want to offend me. He had a bath towel on. When his body started to react to my sensual massage, I saw his amazing shaft. I looked at his dick in awe. I was watching the real pyramid. His dick should be the number one wonder of the world. I did not know that a penis could be that wide.

I knew myself. I am truly prone to addiction. I am addicted to Bill Maher. Well, just watching his show I should say. I could not allow myself to get addicted to Richard De La Chambre's dick. I also could not live the rest of my life wondering about how it feels. I found my way between the horns of the dilemma, my third alternative. I could not waste a magnificent erection; that would just be bad manners. I gave him a blowjob. I pleasured my king and he was happy with his Nefert.

My guitar hero

~

"His hands were clever."

John Steinbeck, *East of Eden*

He fucked me and entered my Hall of Fame. He did not know it at the time, but this was his greatest unrecorded hit. He let his fingers do the talking. These long guitar-playing fingers played my inner woman chord. His fingers played gently, then hard. I felt that we needed to write the rhythm down. I asked if this song had a name. He said, "Stairway to Heaven." I loved the quiet introduction and the chord progression. To this day, I have not heard the song. Now it seems inappropriate. I have lived the song.

You are probably wondering now who is my guitar hero. My dear reader, I will not give him a name. Our American culture loves acronyms. He should be called GH for guitar hero. I will not describe GH either. I grew up believing that describing god was a blasphemy and that belief I kept. Who knew an Arab born-and-raised girl would love rock n' roll? GH gave me the proper introduction and I became a fan.

We met in a French café. It was a business lunch where no business was discussed. In the presence of sexual genius my pussy swam in a sea of daydreams. GH did not tell me that he played the guitar at the time. His deep sensual voice mesmerized me. I gave him a summary of my life. He briefed me on his. Nothing in that life stories exchange explained to me why I felt the way I did. I had this brief moment of clarity where I knew that the meeting had a suspenseful ending. The words "to be continued" appeared white-on-black in my head. I treated my guest to lunch and wished him a safe trip home.

GH emailed me a formal thank-you message for my hospitality. I replied that the pleasure was all mine. I ended that sentence with three dots. I thought, well, if he noticed the extra dots, he would blame my bad English. I had to add the two dots to my sentence to disclose the truth about my wet lunch. I did not eat my fruit bowl that day; instead, I excused myself to the bathroom and tasted my happy juice.

A conference brought GH back to town. We had to have sex. I wanted GH for the same reason sixteenth century poets wrote poetry. I needed to immortalize him into a story. We met on a Wednesday night for dinner. His commanding eyes asked me gently to choose. Raw Sushi was the perfect prelude to raw sex. He gave me the best finger food. He took me on the stairway to heaven. It was the uncut version and no editing required. This song will always remain at the top of my sexual chart.

Phone sex Jared

"There are many rerasons for being skeptics; should we push this skepticism to the very end or stop on the way?"

Henri Poincare, *The value of Science*

I often think of sex as crossing the borders of an individual. Sometimes we let the exotic foreigners in. Then we shortly deport them when the magic dissipates. Until recently, I had been giving only tourist visas. Short sexual recreational visits were all I needed.

My email friend sent me a text to have phone sex. He was bored and I suspected a little drunk. To have phone sex with a person whom I had never been physically with seemed like a leap of faith. For me to take a leap of faith is laughable. I asked myself why I would bother to have phone sex with him. Then the answer came to me; people have phone sex with strangers on 900 numbers every day. I decided, *Well at least it is free. Let's be average for a night.* I called.

My internet friend, whom I would call Jared, answered anxiously. He was Jewish and had the nasal voice. His voice lacked the Sean Connery quality. He said that he had the required experience. I had my doubts. However, I had my bluetooth on already. He started with an oral sex description. I yawned. I told him that I would rather have a woman. He surprised me. He did not get distracted. He did not ask me about my same sex experience. He betrayed his manhood for me. He asked me if a woman would try to possess as she went down on me the way he would. The bad P. word for me is to possess not pussy.

I let Jared infiltrate my lines. I granted him a temporary resident alien status. I made him a prophet. He spoke to me on the mountain of my desire. He took off his shoes on my holy land. He reached the climax of his trance. I nationalized Jared. I announced him my immigrant citizen. Jared remains my internet friend.

F-1 visa

The greatest minds are capable of the greatest vices as well as of the greatest virtues.

Rene Descartes, Discourse on method

Do you know that Muslim men wear a veil? It is called the veil of piety. I proudly corrupted a devout Muslim. I need you to understand he was not a Saudi Muslim. You know that type who crosses the borders to Bahrain every weekend and commits every sin known to man, then goes back home pretending to be pious. He was an Afghan Muslim. You know the kind who comes fresh out of the mountain. I will call him Pashtun. He had his unjustifiable inflated Afghan pride. He gave me the stories straight out of their history books about how Afghanistan is the only nation to defeat all their enemies. Sometimes they survived on eating rocks. He came to the U.S. with a student visa, and boy did he learn? I believe it is called F-1 visa. I told him it meant that he could only fuck one.

Pashtun did not know his real age. His mother told him that he was born the year the snow covered the mountains. In Afghanistan you can issue an identification card with the birthday of your choosing. He chose to be in his early thirties. He looked in his early forties, no doubt due to the harsh conditions of life in Afghanistan. However, he was definitely in his teens if we are talking about emotional age. When he sat next to me, he shivered. He cried when he confessed his love. He was falling very hard, so I had to cushion his fall with my large boobs. He fell for my *hosai stargay*/my gazelle eyes. My erotic poetry drove him over the edge. He called it *Lunday* (anonymous love poems written by Afghan women). He read *Lunday* to me. His favorite one was: "He who comes to my bed has to deposit his heart on the bed as a guarantee." I laughed and told him that it sounded like a rental car agreement. I told him that I had insurance and did not require a deposit. My poems are

17

an x-rated version of *Lunday*. Pashtun said that he always wanted to marry a woman and find out that she wrote *Lunday*. He was disappointed that his wife was illiterate. He said that since he did not get to choose and had met her on their wedding night, the fact she wass illiterate was the least of his disappointments.

He explained to me that although Islam allows divorce, Afghan culture does not allow it. He told me that he had two boys. I eventually found out that he had six children, but in a typical Afghan fashion, the girls were not worth mentioning. He was surprised whenever we discussed any issue because I did not fit his Islamic mold. He insisted on writing a contract before having sex. This practice is called pleasure marriage and Islam allows it as long as the partners do not specify the period of the marriage and there are two male witnesses. In other words, you could be married for an hour or two, a day or two, or indefinitely. I think that it is a wonderful practice for our pro sports players to use; this way the women can't claim rape afterwards. In the contract that he devised carefully, he wrote that I had to promise to love him forever. When I said that forever is a long time, I saw tears in his eyes. At that point, I did not care. I decided that his contract was similar to a user license agreement, and when I download software, I scroll down and hit the (I agree) button. This contract was no different.

He started to demand that I dress in a conservative manner. His friends could not see my legs. He explained that he was jealous because he loved me. I pretended that I had not heard that before from Arab men. I scraped the bottom of my soul to conjure up the leftover Islamic habits. I convinced myself to play the Muslim woman role; after all, there was nothing that I will not do for a good dick.

This is how I started his course of corruption. I wrote a syllabus of the forbidden sex acts in Islam "*Muharamat.*" As a good teacher I needed to know his level of knowledge first, so I asked him to talk about his sex life. When he started to talk about it, I realized that he was at the novice-to-beginner level. He explained that generally children sleep in the same room as the parents. Then after the kids went to sleep, he said that he would wake up his wife to practice his rights. None of that make love crap. He called it "practice his rights." He told me that he was the unusual Afghan and that if his wife complained, he would let her off her duty without hitting her. I asked him why she would complain about being with him. He explained that women wake up very early. They go get water, since most houses do not have running water. They clean the houses and tend to the children. At night, having sex with their husbands is called, "the night chore." He was a nice and sensitive man who allowed his wife to skip the night chore a few times a week, especially on laundry days. I had to ask him how about the children being in the room.

I asked, "Wouldn't the noise wake the children up?"

His eyes were wide open and he said, "What noise? Do women make noise?"

I answered quickly with a very serious face that my vagina sings when she receives. You should have seen the scared look on his face. I was convinced then that my curriculum had to be comprehensive of all his forbidden taboos or "*Muharamat.*"

In Islam, women have to wax because hair can't meet hair. Although my personal preference is a nice Brazilian with a small landing strip, I am not a fan of the required aspect of waxing in Islam. I am not a fan of the required anything. He had to wait two months for our first time, and my pussy grew a beard for my devout Muslim.

He had never seen his wife of twelve years naked. Our first date had to be a strip club. Instead of a drink, I bought him a lap dance. The girl I picked looked eatable and he would not let her dance for him. I slapped her on her ass and put a large tip in her g-string. It is quite the scene when your date refuses the lap dance. People at the club looked at me escorting my fag outside. He started crying and mumbled something about respecting me. Later on, he explained that he was really just afraid of Aids. It was really hard to refrain from laughing, so I kissed him instead.

In Islam, if the woman has her period her husband will not touch her. In Afghanistan, he explained that they take a step farther; the wife would sleep in the guest room during her period. I decided that it was time for my Pashtun to meet blood. I made him wait. He used British swearing words and our first time was bloody awesome.

On our second time when I got on my knees to give him a blowjob, he did not know what I was doing. Later he told me that it was his first blowjob and that women in Afghanistan do not do that. I had my Aha moment. I figured out what we needed to do to liberate the women in Afghanistan. Charter a plane of female volunteers and teach Afghan women how to give blowjobs. That would be worthy of a Red Cross mission and it would definitely give them the upper hand.

I tried to introduce him to the term 'quickie' but that term did not translate well in Pashto. The fresh air in the mountains gave him raw talent. Graduation day came when I introduced him to the back door. He performed well in all other taboos or "*Muharamat*" and this was his final test. I said he either passed or risked not having sex with me again. Of course, that was an ultimatum he could not take. He followed my step-by-step instructions. I gave him an A for Anal. We finished all the lessons and all the extra curricular activities such as watching porn, watching me masturbate, having sex in the office, in a car, and on the beach. He got extra credit for skype sex because it was his first time to masturbate. My devout Muslim lost his veil. Once the veil dropped, there was no mystery. He was no longer pure and I was no longer interested.

Indoor Mark

∾

The tragedy of sexual intercourse is the perpetual virginity of the soul.

William Yeats

Sex is my religion. If you want to know one thing and only one thing about Arabs, you should know they take their religion seriously. I met Mark at Starbucks one day. He held the door open for me. I did not think, 'what a gentleman.' I wondered what sex would be like with him. He bought me my soy latte. We talked briefly. I don't remember what he said. I had the picture on pause so the voice was on mute. He was sitting across from me, but in my mind I was on top. Why do they have such comfortable chairs at Starbucks? We exchanged phone numbers. I did not text him 'see you later.' My text was, "Fuck you later!"

Mark was born and raised in California. The sun took liberty on his skin. Arabic culture exalts age. I am always turned on by older-looking men. To me he looked perfect. The next day, I told the story to my girlfriends. My closest girlfriend, Safiya, asked jokingly, "Really, an Ajax white guy is that sexy?" I explained that he must have had a fatal accident and got a Moroccan blood transfusion. A lot of it, I presume.

Our first and last outdoor date was on the pier to see the sunset. He was talking about a green flash thing. I did not understand what he said. I just wanted him to stop talking. I kissed him. We made out for hours. I was reclaiming a teenage life that had been robbed from me by my culture. He walked me to my car. I asked him to follow me home or did I follow him? Details … details … we stole fire from Earth; in other words, we had sex.

Mark does not have a dick. He has the key to my box. Sex with Mark was the type of sex that makes you climb mountains and defy the Olympian gods. I should know. I slept with Zeus once! Sex with Mark had an earthquake quality. It destroyed what existed before

21

it and shook me to my core. Afterwards, I had tremors for hours and sometimes for days. He had it all: the older man's looks and the younger man's stamina.

Mark became indoor Mark! Why would I meet him outside and lose valuable fucking time? My girlfriends warned me and asked me to slow down. One girlfriend pointed out that I did not know if Mark flirted with waitresses. I did not care. Honestly, if he flirted with a waitress, I would ask her to join. What Mark wants, Mark gets!

Before him, I was a strong woman. It turned out that I was a piñata. Once he hit me as hard as he did, all kind of pink candies came out. Indoor Mark became my drug! For the first time in my life, I missed a man. I knew that the gods would not allow this kind of sex to persist. My intensity scared him. I guess that I can explain what happened by cultural differences. It is the difference between soccer and baseball. When you score in soccer, you make your goal. You celebrate. In baseball, when you hit, you have to run and he did.

Days passed … or had it been months? It felt like years. I sent him a text: "My pussy misses you." Indoor Mark became my on demand/pay per view! Well, no pay, just my hurt feelings when he no longer walks me to my car.

Meet Frank the frank

"Some say pleasure is the highest good, while others maintain that it is thoroughly bad."

Aristotle, *Ethics*

The expression is "boy meets girl," but in reality it is boy meets rubber, then rubber meets girl. Dating is a social disease and everyone is infected. I met Frank on the website 'Plenty of fish.' The name explains the whole premise: everyone has several options. I devised a clever profile, calling myself the catch of everyday. Frank asked me what I wanted. He said that if I wanted someone to wine and dine me, he was not my guy. He even read me my rights and the non-exclusivity statement. It baffled me that he would bother to say it so early. Is it not the golden rule of the dating game? I was not sure why he had to read me the fine print. Needless to say, he was a character I had to meet.

Dating is like playing musical chairs and very few men know how to play this game. Most men run around and around. In the middle of the game, even if a man meets the perfect seat, very few men stop. When the music stops each man picks the nearest seat. When Frank played the game the first time around he secured a seat early on. Then three years later, he realized he was not comfortable in it. He sold it in a yard sale and never looked back.

Frank was creative or so it seemed. He found a solution. The friends with benefits system was too time-consuming for him. He invented the Fuck without benefits. Every new idea is really an old idea revisited. Frank's idea was no different. The Fuck without benefits is really a modern-life bartering system and that system is as old as humanity.

In all his forthrightness, he managed to be the most evasive person. He told me that women found his honesty refreshing. He mentioned that among his female exploits he had an FBI agent.

Of course, if you offer nothing you can only attract women who are successful and self-sufficient. I am not really sure that he had them. It was probably the other way around; they had him. He offered himself. He got picked by cheap cougars who did not want to pay. I looked myself in the mirror. I asked myself if I should deliver for Frank and compete with all the other successful women who deliver. Would he attach my number with a magnet to the fridge? I knew that I could deliver it hot. I knew that I could include more toppings than all other competitors. Between the ways I use my hands to knead the dough, the different taste and the extra toppings, I can win any competition.

That was not what I wanted. I wanted a boyfriend who would take me to the Super Bowl game party like other couples. Not that I understand football or really cared about it. How could I call myself American if I have never been invited to a Super Bowl party? I just feel like my naturalization is not complete. I swore to forsake all other countries. I got myself an ex like every true American. Now, the only thing missing was an invitation for a Super Bowl party.

Frank was a handsome young man. I was tempted. He was sexually charged and I loved that about him. He sent me a picture text with his morning wood and said: "Wood morning!" I thought, well, I could start my unmentionable list with him. My girlfriend Karen told me that every woman has an unmentionable list and that is why when asked about the number of partners the number is divided by two or three.

I decided not to fuck Frank and not because he was frank. I write stories about my partners so I could not have an unmentionable list. According to yahoo maps, he lived twenty-five minutes away. I thought that he should get his sex delivery from a closer local provider.

Short

の

"Since our senses sometimes deceive us, I decided to suppose that nothing exactly was as our senses would have us imagine."
                                        Rene Descartes, Discourse on method

I had an orgasm in self defense. I could not really tell the man that his knife could not cut melted butter. Dating is no longer about finding a mate for me. It is more about adding a controlled dose of excitement to my life. I find it funny, all the little ways men remind women that it is just dating. Sometimes, I feel like telling the guy, "Hey, I promise to get bored before you do."

I think that I understand most of the code words: "I have been really selective" — translation: It has been a while and you should expect a short ride. "I take care of my woman first," — translation: Something is wrong with my instrument and I compensate. "Women beg me to stop" — translation: I am really boring and women can't feign interest. "I heard good things about the blue pill" — translation: Run! That was another digression, my apologies just leftover Arab culture in my soul. Let me get back to my story and tell you how I get myself in that self defense situation.

I entered his house. The furniture looked more like props from *That 70s Show*. A dusty brown macramé greeted me at the door. Fiber optics lamps were in charge of the living room. I was sure that the disco ball would drop down at any minute. Once again I chose a man who was 6 feet tall. When would I learn that the size of instrument had nothing to do his shoes size or nose size like Arabs believe? It is not his fault that he is 6 foot and 2 inches tall who comes up short at delivery time. Now I know why we use the verb blow; his instrument was the size of a whistle.

Short was a gracious host. He took me outside to see the backyard. He bragged about having a large yard. I had a feeling that

I did not want to be there on Halloween. I heard voices coming from beyond the ground.

One woman's voice said, "I was rude. Don't be rude to him!"

Another woman's voice gave me advice. She said, "Whatever you do, do not laugh!" I had the urge to flee that unmarked crime scene. Then I decided, what kind of adventurer I would be. The choice was clear: either large yard or pretend short was large. I could not join these ladies and I followed the advice given to me by their spirits. I had to summon the spirit of Meg Ryan in *When Harry Met Sally* to moan and scream. I saw a flickering light and he claimed that the smoke alarm battery was going bad. I pretended that there was a hidden camera and so I must put on a worthy show. Yes, my orgasm was in self-defense. To some extent, the perceived danger enticed me. I was sincere when I kissed Short good night.

H 1 B visa

"You can boast about anything if it is all you have. Maybe the less you have the more you are required to boast."

John Steinbeck, *East of Eden*

"This has never happened to me before," said the one-minute man. I lay naked in bed chained by the rules of politeness. I could have said, "at least twice with me," but I did not. I stood up and got dressed. This was the last time I saw Jose. Let me tell you how I let my first Hispanic man inside my borders.

Jose was not tall. He was maybe 5 foot 8. The image that we have of our preferred mate gets formulated at a very young age. For me to allow a man on my ride, he had to meet the minimum required height of 6 feet or he would cry at the gate. When Jose first approached me, he applied for an H1 B visa. It is a working visa for an extended period of time. In fact, he was so sure of his expertise. "I am a pleaser," he said. He sent me a picture of him sticking his tongue out which gave me nightmares. He assured me that I would grant him my green card. He claimed to be the best professional in pleasing women. He said that his equipment measured 9 inches. I laughed and told him that it was a little hard to swallow.

I decided to set up an interview period to see if I should grant him a visa. I required three reference letters from previous fuck partners who were willing to vouch for him. His answer was Hispanic men are *Caliente*. He told me that I could ask any woman and just watch TV. He submitted his application without any letters of reference. I did not give him the call for the interview.

He wanted to get erected. He started a campaign for his dick. He sent me a hundred and twenty messages a day. His propaganda flooded my inbox. I hoped his dick would flood my box. He wrote things right out of porn movies. "I want to spank that ass while my

27

balls are slapping your pussy." "I want you to hop on my cock and bounce those gorgeous tits on my face." He did not use the female romance language which men speak fluently to attract women. I liked that. He addressed me in the right language. I am multilingual, but sex is the only language that I like to teach. It is the most widely spoken language and Rosetta stone should add new software to teach it. His campaign paid off. It made me crave him. I finally replied with a one-line message. I wrote, "You got my vote."

I invited him to eat sushi. He put a condition. He said that he would eat sushi only if he got my pussy for dessert. I got the sushi to go. Jose met me at my house. I had gotten permission for an extended lunch. He ate and ate. I was more than ready to hoist the flag, however it was a mourning day. He apologized. He said that he was too excited to finally have me. I used the time I had left to go for a jog. I needed to jog. Jose did have a working knowledge of the language. However when he practiced I did not like his accent. I wanted to put him in a remedial immersion class. I could not just give up on a student right away.

He asked me out of dinner. I said that lunch was better for me. I figured why waste an evening for a make-up class. Again, he was genuinely a pleaser. He spent twenty to thirty minutes south of the border and one minute to cross it. I wanted to call the border patrol on his ass. I realized that my first Hispanic man only needed a temporary field working visa, not an H1 B visa. He said that next time we should have Mexican food. I figured maybe he needed taco reinforcements to get his *caliente* quality.

Against my better judgment, I decided to accept his Mexican lunch invitation. I could not kiss him after he had his onion-filled burritos, so he went down to business. He started his routine. Then the one-minute man had a good thirty seconds of glory. That was the last time I met Jose. I denied Jose's H1B visa application. I told him that I reconciled with my ex-boyfriend. That was my first brown lie. Oral sex is a nice appetizer, but I am really a main course type of girl. I have to doubt the tales of the *caliente* quality of Hispanic men. If any of the rumors were true, then why did I have the one-minute microwave oven hot. I started to wonder about the expression 'no way Jose.' Could it be that a number of women were not pleased by a number of men called Jose?

The stunt double

∽

"How useless is painting, which attracts admiration by the resemblance of things, the originals of which we do not admire!"

Pascal, *Pensees*

Sex for men is about the finish line, but for women it is about the race, and damn it, they will have to come first. A week ago, I got a message from a man who wanted to meet me. He read my profile online and wanted to see if he could be the star of my happily-ever-after story. He did not comment on my slutty-looking pictures; he was interested in what I wrote. I was intrigued and had to meet him. He was as tall as Sean Connery with Daniel Craig's build and yummy ass. You can take his picture from any angle and enjoy the view. The only thing to remember is to skip the face. It seemed only fitting to call him he stunt double or SD for short.

I met SD for coffee in a bistro. The waitress was beautiful. When a beautiful woman asks you what you want for food, you don't just answer, "I am here for coffee." You ask for a moment and look at the menu. SD asked me how come a beautiful woman like me was not married. I answered that I just did not like leftovers and no matter how good the food is, I don't take it home. See my dear reader, once the food is presented to you, it comes the way your order it. If you take it home, everything changes. It is wrapped in plastic or foil, or a plastic or foam container; yuck. Sometimes it spills on the way. It is never going to look the same at home. Even if the food retains some of the original flavors, how long can you really expect to reheat, eat, and still pretend to enjoy it?

At this point of the conversation, he was intrigued. By definition, I was every man's dream: beautiful, smart, and not into commitment. SD was a naval officer. How appetizing. I have a weakness for those ring knockers. Naval officers are taught strategies at the Academy. I decided to ambush his king with my queen. He moved

29

his bishop and started the mental game. I had a lazy start and only moved a pawn. I wanted him to entertain me first. He started to tell about his family back in Chicago. I started to imagine him dancing for me. I gave him the necessary nod to continue talking. SD asked me if he passed the chemistry test. I told him that there was a required question of kissing. We ended our meal and went for a walk.

I told my friend Safiya that I was planning on kissing my date. She warned me not to kiss him on a first date. Safiya always has my best interest at heart. She gave me the hunter speech. The man has to hunt and it is all about the pursuit. Safiya started to threaten me with giving me the nickname *hot lips*. I liked that nickname. I told Safiya that was either to fuck or kiss on a first date. It had been a while for me. When I saw how his body was cut of steel, I thought why choose; I decided to kiss him, then fuck him.

We sat on park bench and kissed for an hour. SD was very passionate. He moaned as I kissed him. I wanted to give him a short preview of what I would do to his dick. I kissed his upper lip, then lathered it with saliva. I massaged his tongue with my tongue front to back.

I stroked the sides with long and quick touches. I let his tongue touch the back of my throat. I wanted him to know that I would take his dick all in. I held his face with one hand and grazed his thigh with the other hand. I felt that I was winding the box, but Jack did not come out.

I was suddenly reminded of something that I had to do at home. He tried to get me to stay. I did not make out with him and left him hanging. I left him because there was no evidence of his hanging. I saw the end screen coming down. I do not normally wait for the movie credits; even when they try to entertain the audience and add the bloopers, I still leave. SD is not going to get a call back. You can't cast a stunt double in a main role.

Business as usual

~~

We never live; we are always in the expectation of living.

Voltaire

He entered my office as if no other man had entered my office before. If you knew where I worked you would find that funny. I work at MGC (Man Grand Central Station) where every five minutes there is a man, a handsome man, at the door. I apologize to Dr. Seuss, but here we have white man, yellow man, brown man, black man, tall man, short man, big man, small man, young man, and old man. They are all healthy and handsome men. When he entered my office, it felt different. It was not a forced entry, but he might as well have kicked the door down. He knocked at the door the same way policemen announce their entry in cops show. He asked me for a form, but all my hormones heard was, "I demand attention and before me a woman you should kneel."

He sat across from me. I blamed myself for wearing a dress that day. I had always asked my female co-workers why they wore pants all the time. I do not think that I got an honest answer. At 10:15 on a Wednesday morning, sitting across from him, I got my answer. It is not to look professional, but rather act professional. Women wear pants at work to prevent those easy access moments where all you think about is jumping on a business associate's lap. He started small talk, which immediately turned into big talk. He asked me how I grew up, not where I grew up.

Do men really know what they are doing? When you feign interest in the woman's life, when you listen attentively, when you act like you really care, it is the equivalent of fluffing the woman. How would you like it if I came into your office, unzipped your pants, and sucked your cock? You would love it and that is what I did: I loved it.

I decided to occupy my hands with a pen. Unintentionally, I started to stroke it. Well, that did not really work. I put the pen down. It was not my fault. Someone should have named his biceps or at least put up a sign on these large borders of his torso town. He made a size 12 woman feel like a size 6 wanting to disappear between his arms. My hormones started the mating dance. I yelled at my hormones and asked them to behave. My hormones whispered, "He would perfect for that rape fantasy you have always had." My body was mad at my professional demeanor. It gave me a red card. It did. It slapped me down with my period unexpectedly.

I wanted to ask about all his different tattoos, but I decided that it would be too risky. With every story behind every tattoo, I would make a quilt of stories, and voila, my perfect man would be across from me. I am a woman who builds the man's image to be something I want before I ever get to know him. Safiya had warned me about this habit. I decided that this time I would not. I would let him come and leave with just his form, business as usual.

Suicide sex mission

Cease to think that the decrees of the gods can be changed by prayers.

Virgil

The only constant thing in life is change. I hold this sentence to be the third and last axiom of life. If you do not remember the first two axioms, I hereby sentence you to read my stories again. This time pay attention and do not get excited. Indoor Mark ended our relationship game after only one inning. He called the game off because of a bad weather forecast. After the end of our relationship, I was only contacting him for booty calls. For him, it was a booty call and for me it was an ER visit. My pussy had a hard time breathing without his dick. The last time I contacted him asking if I could fuck him he answered, "maybe." He pitched me a slider and I stood there puzzled and frozen. This word was my pussy's death sentence. He should have asked me to stand up. He should have recited all my crimes of passion. It was karma in action, my punishment for ridiculing love and crushing Jason's heart.

I am Arab born and raised, hardwired for extreme feelings. Mark brought out that intensity in me. He did not just fuck me, he penetrated my sealed heart. My love for him was that all-consuming love described in Rumi's poems. His "maybe" activated my violent sleeper cell DNA. I needed to self-destruct. I could not imagine myself allowing another man to fuck me. It would be suicide, I thought. Then I decided suicide it must be.

I decided to bury my love and longing for Mark in any brief, meaningless intercourse. I was sexually fully charged so I just needed an innocent bystander to explode on him. I went online to chat and find a horny victim. No man could ever measure up to my idea of Indoor Mark, so I decided to fuck the most despicable man. I had to devise a lie. I chatted with the first local man online. I told him that I was married. I said that my husband was in Iraq.

I figured a man who is willing to sleep with a spouse of a military member has to be despicable. He wanted to meet for lunch and get a room with the fisherman special in a motel by the water. I thought that lunch was pointless, since there was nothing this man could say that would make me want to fuck him or stop me from completing my suicide sex mission. That day, I woke up with one idea consuming me to seek martyrdom for the sake of Mark.

Green is the color of Islam and it is the color most worn on suicide missions. I bought a sleazy green dress that whores would refuse to wear. The kind of dress you need Halloween to justify wearing it. I went for my suicide sex mission. I met Andrew, if that indeed was his name, last Christmas. He said that he was spreading joy for five women. I laughed. I told him that even Muslims are not allowed to keep more than four wives. Andrew's looks were the definition of average in a Webster dictionary. I was a little puzzled. I paid for the room and we went for lunch. I told him that since I was going to fuck him anyway, he could talk about whatever he liked.

He started the small talk by saying that I was two dress sizes away from his type. I did not comment. I asked him to show me pictures of his women. He did. He had pictures of his women on his phone. He had one white, one Hispanic, and three black women. The one common denominator was they were all overweight. I initially thought that he meant I was two dress sizes bigger than his type. It turned out that I was two sizes smaller. I told him that we all have our preferred types. He said that he did not prefer bigger women, but rather, he specialized in the queen size. I guess for him, I was just a full size, not a queen. I asked him to elaborate. He said that men call bigger women, "the grateful kind." I realized that I did manage to find the most despicable man. I got really quiet as he started to explain how he normally found his women on that big beautiful women website. His monologue had the same quality of a slim fast drink. It was tasteless, but necessary. His speech was like electric shock therapy that snapped me out of my depression. I decided to abort my sexual suicide mission. I handed him the key to the room. I thanked him. I told him to order porn on me which he did. Andrew speech was so effective that I did not gain my regular ten pounds holiday weight. In fact, I lost ten pounds. No pecan pie could ever erase the memory of his five women's pictures.

I went to see my friend Safiya and confessed my failed suicide attempt. Safiya is a white American female friend. I gave her the nickname Safiya because she is pure of heart. I am not a believer in Christianity. However, there is something to be said about a religion that makes its followers the most accepting and forgiving people.

Safiya decided to take me on a healing trip to Huntington Beach. She said that indoor Mark was my Mr. Big and I was young Carrie. I just needed a trip to move on and forget Mr. Big. Safiya felt guilty. She said that she predisposed me to fall for Mark. A year ago, she has described Huntington Beach as the Promised Land for those women who like white men. She said that most men get the premature signs of aging from constant exposure to the sun. I do not think that I fell for Mark only because of his wrinkles. The fact that he happened to be from Huntington Beach did not play a role either. Nevertheless, I decided to go man hunting in Huntington Beach.

We spent the weekend with her loving family. Her parents are a happy couple who celebrated fifty-three years of happy marriage. Their hospitality had an Arab-like feel. They took us for breakfast at the Sugar Shack. As I watched this loving couple share their meal, I knew that I might have lost my indoor Mark, but there is life after Mark. Couples like her parents are the reason we celebrate Valentine's Day and join dating websites. Safiya and I agree that they are the exception, not the rule.

I knew that I might get another Mark. This time he would have to be an outdoor Mark. I would fly with him to Huntington Beach to have breakfast at the Sugar Shack. I have been on a good man diet since this trip. Men don't come with nutritional facts so following the diet is hard. I used to fall for the polysaturated evil man. Sometimes, on a Wednesday a man comes around the office and I can sense a man in heat. I crave humping but I resist. Sometimes, I want to cheat on my diet and reach for the closest horny dog. It is not really a good diet since it is based on starvation. It is more like fasting. I had the fasting Ramadan training since I was seven-years-old. Fasting Ramadan might mess up with your kidney function, but will no doubt give you endurance. I decided to follow my fast and find myself an outdoor Mark.

35

Her Layla

"... that gender is a choice, or that gender is a role, or that gender is a construction that one puts on, as one puts on clothes in the morning, that there is a 'one' who is prior to this gender, a one who goes to the wardrobe of gender and decides with deliberation which gender it will be today."

Judith Butler, *Gender Trouble:*
Feminism and the Subversion of Identity

I pleasured my first Saudi woman ten years ago. She was beautiful so I will call her Jameela. Any other name would be an insult to her beauty. She was tall with long, jet black silky hair. She was skinny, as she did not have the child-bearing hips that Arab women traditionally have. She was one of four ladies who lived in the same apartment complex. They all wore the black Abaya, which is the traditional tent covering Arab women's bodies. I saw them around the laundromat. They never saw me as they always looked down. My American friend Jennifer pointed and said the penguins are walking.

One day an Arab man approached me in the parking lot and asked if I would like to meet his wife. He explained that they lived in the apartment building behind me. He said that all the men were leaving their wives for two months to go in the field with their American counterparts. He explained that since none of the wives worked, they needed help with groceries for the children while their husbands were away. I could not refuse to help. Some of them had children and when Arabs call on each other to help the only acceptable answer is yes. I agreed to meet the wives and take care of their needs. Only at the time, I did not realize that meant all their needs.

I was invited to a dinner where I was introduced to the four families. When I went I felt overdressed until the men left the apartment to go play backgammon in another apartment. Men and women do not hang out together in Arab countries. As soon as the men ate, they left. The women dropped their veils. They were dressed in the latest French designer clothing. I had a great evening that night. They put on Arabic music and three of the five of us danced. One woman did not dance. She did not even smile to warm bread, as we say about people who are sour all the time. They tied their scarves around their hips. Jameela put her scarf on my hips and I danced. They all gave me the same compliment that I danced well and that I reminded them of Layla Elwy. She is a beautiful Egyptian actress. In American terms, a size 12 Kim Kardashian. Jameela gave me her scarf that night because I liked it. We were in her apartment and she did not need it to leave. You have to be careful when you compliment Arabs; they tend to insist on offering the object to you. It seemed only appropriate to put a picture of that scarf on the cover of my book.

I started to get the groceries for the woman. They would call me day or night to buy things for them. That lasted ten days or so before they asked me if they could clean my place and make me dinner. I had a full-time job, so adding on the responsibility to buy them groceries was not easy. However, coming back home to a clean apartment and home-cooked meal was great. Each of the four wives took turns bringing food and cleaning my place before I came back.

One night I came back and found Jameela at my place. She had her veil on and was about to leave my apartment. I joked with her saying, "Honey, I am home." She did not understand the joke. When I explained that is what a husband says when he comes home, she laughed and played along. She said that I looked stressed and she needed to give me a massage. I told her that was her Arabic duty. She looked at me seriously and ordered me to go to the bedroom and get ready for the massage. I was actually tired and stressed that day. I got undressed and went for a quick shower. I went under the covers. Jameela came into the room. She took off her veil and when her veil dropped she was a wild woman. She started to massage my back gently. Then she used her fingernails and lightly scratched my back. I was getting a little undone. She got on top of my ass and started to massage me with her long black hair. At this point, I had to stop her and ask what was going on. She started to cry. She told me that she loved me. I could not really respond. It was so shocking that I lost my ability to speak. She explained that Saudi girls are raised in isolation from the boys. She said that where she grew in Taif, everyone got together and pleasured each other. The unspoken rule was they had to stop once they got married. She had been with other girls before her marriage. She told me everything about her loveless arranged marriage. Every night she would offer herself to her husband and initiate sex as decreed by Islam. Her husband would finish as quickly as he could, then jump in the shower without talking to her at all. He had to follow the *Tahara* rule of cleansing after sex, but she could not get her husband to cleanse before sex. She added that Islam ordered the man to speak to the woman. She always defended Islam.

Girls in Egypt, Morocco, and Lebanon are not raised in isolation from boys. I did not know about that secret practice in Saudi. I used to think of Saudi as the pure Saudi until I met Saudis. She put my hand on her pearly breast. She asked me to touch her. She asked me to give her a chance with tears in her eyes.

I could not deny Jameela. She had become a good friend. I felt bad hearing about her bad situation. Plus my pussy was flooding form her sensual massage. She used her scarf and used it to blindfold me. She asked me not to think of her. I smiled. She went down on me. I finally understood the benefit behind ululating, the ugly barbaric sound that Arab women make. Ululating is not only a sign of victory. It is how women achieve victory. My pussy squirted in her mouth. She swallowed my cum. I took the blindfold off and kissed her. She tasted well … like me. I learned that I like the taste of pussy. It was my turn. She did not ask me for anything, but I could not just be a taker. I took Sean out the night stand. She looked horrified. She asked me what I wanted to do with it. I asked her to trust me. I put the blindfold on her. I fucked her with Sean nice and slow. She was moaning quietly. I ordered her to scream and call my name. She started to say *Nicknee*/fuck me. Jameela spent the night at my place.

We went to take a shower together. She washed my back and my hair. I kissed every inch of her beautiful body. We went to sleep and I held her all night. When I explained that it was called cuddling, she looked at me and said that she loved the English language for having this verb. I did not realize it at the time but she called me Layla all night.

In the morning before I left for work I playfully leaned against the bed and put twenty dollars bill next to her. I said jokingly, "For you, my *sharmoota*/whore." She asked me to call her *Gahaba*/whore in Gulf Arabic as she pulled me back to bed. She said that she had to earn it. She put her hands on my ass and massaged it. Then she went down and started to kiss, then lick my ass. I could not believe how pleasurable that felt. She taught me how and my partners after her all thanked Jameela in absentia for her lesson. She explained that this was a Saudi treat, that a Saudi wife literally kissed her husband's ass after sex to show gratitude. In Arabic the "kiss my ass" translates into "*Telhass Teezee*/lick my ass." I guess the kissing is customary but the licking is extra.

As I was leaving the apartment she asked me if she could come after my work. All my Saudi friends were rotating days to cook for me. Jameela decided that the only one to take care of me should be her. I did not mind.

I did not plan on having Jameela stay in my place for almost two months while her husband was away, but her ass-licking skills sold me. She could not believe that I was willing to kiss and lick her ass. She said that as a woman she was unworthy to receive the pleasure. I asked her to never again say unworthy in front of me. She obeyed.

Jameela was an amazing woman of rare beauty. I asked her if she had Asian blood. She was a little ashamed to tell me. Her mother was a Philippino maid. The help in the house do the chores in the morning, but at night if the husband decides to use the maid sexually, whether consensual or not, he can. Her mother was only fifteen when she got pregnant with her. Her father kept the baby and returned the mother to her country. She grew up thinking that her stepmother was her mother. She could not understand why she was treated so poorly until one day in a verbal fight her sister called the "maid's daughter."

Jameela and I got along and had no disagreements except one day. Sanaa, another Saudi woman in the group, called me one day at work and asked me to go to her house for an emergency. I got worried that something happened to one of her children. I left my work in a hurry. When I arrived at her door, she greeted me with a negligee. I pushed her in. I demanded an explanation. She said that Jameela bragged about my large nipples and big areolas. I could not believe it, but three out of the four women wanted to fuck me. Now that I was with Jameela the other two were jealous. Sanaa said that she came from a bigger family and that she had her own family money to use at her discretion.

I was insulted when she showed me a fatwa allowing her to seek comfort in other women while her husband is away. Fatwa is a religious decree that a Muslim Imam announces. Technically any Muslim can fund the research of a fatwa and seek the opinion of a Muslim Imam on any topic.

That sheik used verses saying that the ultimate sin is for the woman to cheat on her husband and somehow came to the conclusion that any other means are allowed. This fatwa was probably the Cadillac of all crazy fatwa (s). I asked her, "How much did funding this bullshit of a fatwa cost?" I said sarcastically that she could have paid me directly. Without hesitation, she said, "Whatever you want, you are worth your weight in gold to me." Given my weight, that is a lot of money, I tell you. I apologized to Sanaa and told her that I was not in the fucking women business. I did not want her black oil money. I still think that oil money stains the soul.

Sanaa insulted Jameela. She called her the maid's daughter and a barren womb as she had no children. I got offended. I told Sanaa sarcastically that maybe if she included her husband I would consider her. She looked terrified. She started to beg to never mention anything to her husband. She said that she could never let her husband know that she liked me. She assured me that he would divorce her immediately. The attitude of Arab men is a little different than American men. They would not like it if their wives asked to add a girlfriend to the equation. They get insulted and think that it is an insult to their manhood. I realized that I scared her by mentioning her husband. I apologized and promised not to tell her husband. She ran into the bedroom and brought the Koran. She asked me to swear on it that I would never tell her husband. I did. Swearing on the Koran remains the only guarantee that a Muslim will not lie. I left her feeling guilty.

41

I went home and yelled at Jameela for the first and last time. She was in tears. I melted at the sight of her tears. She was naked, as she liked to walk naked in my apartment. Her body was shivering. Her smooth areolas punched up and her nipples got aroused whenever she cried. She said that she would understand if I chose Sanaa over her or if I wanted to add Sanaa. She got on the floor and kissed my feet, apologizing. I held her up. I kissed her. I took her to the bathroom and drew a calming bath for her. I asked her not to brag to the other ladies about my nipples and what we do. There was no point in hurting anyone's feelings. I promised Jameela that I would only be her Layla. I bought some sex toys for the other two ladies. I showed them how to use them on each other, then went back home aroused for my beautiful Jameela.

Jameela was a devout Muslim. She did not miss a prayer and hated that I did not pray with her. I could not pray with her because I got turned on watching her pray. She cried reading the Koran and every time she cried I knew that her nipples are aroused and waiting for my lips. The only thing I hated about Jameela was her alarm. She had this awful sounding alarm which blared Allah Akbar every hour.

My relationship lasted six months before she had to leave. She gave me a twenty-one karat gold ring to remind me of her. She bought me a French perfume called *J'adore*/I adore. She made me swear on the Koran not to use it for another woman. The company came up with a new version called *J'adore l'eau*/I adore the water. I thought of trying it. Technically, it is not the same perfume; then I decided to keep my promise to Jameela. After all, I was her Layla.

Sexual pilgrimage

I slept with God — or Paul, if you want to know God's name. He is white, by the way, but he hated how white he was so he used tanning beds. What do you know; he does dwell among us! With my guitar hero, I knew that I was with a man who had reached deity level. When Paul fucked — and I mean he really fucked me — I said, "Oh God," addressing him, not an imaginary being in the sky.

I started my sexual pilgrimage with some necessary sexual rituals. I observed a sexual fast for four months. Earlier that day, I waxed my pussy. I cut two inches of my hair. I reached into my sexual fantasies closet and chose a black-and-white French maid outfit with a black apron. I also took out my white bathrobe, which I had bought on sale from Victoria's Secret. It stayed new in my closet for a year. I was not sure why I took it out that day, as if I knew on a subconscious level that this was my pilgrimage. White is the color required for pilgrims. For Paul/God, I picked a blue bathrobe that matched his gorgeous eyes. I anointed his body with Arnica oil from the trees of Morocco. I chose aromatic candles with eucalyptus scent to light the room. I bought a dark chocolate for us to share a sin of pleasure after we consummated our first sin.

I needed a sexual pilgrimage to get absolved from my sins. After several weak partners, my sexual identity was getting polluted. I was becoming a castrating feminist. It all started by my constant desire to be the woman on top. The power became my addiction. I stripped most of my past lovers of their control. The more I took the lead, the more they liked it. Before I knew it, I was the dominant partner in bed. Many times, I left my partners feeling crippled, powerless, inadequate, and above all, happily dominated. I gave instructions. I took charge of changing positions. I turned animal and devoured each sexual partner. I stomped on their manhood one man at a time. That was my life before Paul and before the pilgrimage.

As I anointed Paul with oil, I saw a birthmark on his upper left thigh. I knew that he was God. He was the man with the capital

43

letter M. I had seen this birthmark years ago. I understood that he came to my bed to restore my faith in men. I spared him my emasculating sexual behaviors. I wanted to be the submissive partner. I wanted to feel vulnerable to the overpowering man. I lay back and enjoyed the joy that only a man can give. He did not disappoint me. He expressed himself the way a god should. His dick rattled the walls of my pussy. He reclaimed the assertiveness which I had previously stolen from most of my past lovers.

Paul whisked me on a journey to Jerusalem. He took me to bathe in the eternal sexual fountain. He washed my body. His dick tenderized my hardened pussy and my pussy went to sleep happy. Paul absolved me from my dominant woman's sins. He asked me if I had always been the woman on top. I answered him smiling that maybe I was. As I confessed my previous sins, the atonement was complete. My body testified his shihada/testimony of faith. My pussy swore that there is no god, but God and Paul is his messenger, created in his image.

The happy meal

"When I had first become inflamed with a passion for wisdom and had resolved that, once I found it, I would leave behind me all the empty hopes and deceitful frenzies of vain desires."

St. Augustine, *The confessions of St. Augustine*

I looked young Tim in the eyes and asked him if I could buy him a happy meal. He laughed. What a beautiful laugh he had! He answered yes and added that he passed the happy meal age requirement. I asked him when he was born. He said October 25th, 1985. I smiled. There must be a special place in hell reserved for a woman born in 1973 who wants to fuck a man born in 1985. However, I wanted to serve young Tim the happiest meal. It is all about the toy! And boy, he was going to enjoy my toy box. I thought that young Tim deserved the full course Arabic meal starting with the belly dancing appetizer, followed by a sensual massage, a side of all-I-can-suck, gourmet-tasting pussy and ass-licking dessert. I went home and talked to my friend.

He said, "Samara, you are too broke to be a cougar, or is it a puma at your age?" Apparently, if I am in my thirties and forties then I am just a puma, not a cougar. Should I abandon the young Tim fantasy for fear of getting an animal name? I had to ask myself. After all, I am Arab and animal names do not scare me. I have been called gazelle for my eyes; now I would just turn into a puma.

This is how it started. Young Tim joined our work group. I did not pay attention to him at first. He did not fit my lover profile. He looked like a young Mr. Frodo. No, I am not talking about his feet. The similarity resided in the innocent blue eyes. This young Frodo had not left the shire yet. My friend Safiya, whom I adore and respect, started talking about young Tim. She called him smart and genuinely a good guy. I believe that Safiya placed young Tim in my head. Young Tim was her crush. I love Safiya so much I gave her the only girlfriend veto right. If she did not like a man I dated, she could veto him and boot him off my island. She did not like indoor Mark but she tolerated my infatuation for him.

Remember, my dear reader, my sexual identity was polluted. I wrote my stories to exfoliate the dead sexual and sinful skin. I had started to follow my spiritual sex fast. Was young Tim worth breaking a yearlong celibacy oath? It is more of an academic year, a nine months sabbatical for analyzing and reflection. My work friend Mikayla concurred he was worth it. She said, "Well, Samara, look at his rosy cheeks."

I had to laugh at her German comment. I did not notice his rosy cheeks. That is what I call a cultural difference. I looked at his other cheeks, which were the perfect size and looked perfectly lick-able. Safiya said that young Tim did not get the MAT (Men Asshole Training) yet. The MAT is a training that Safiya and I believe most men get during their thirties. I had to agree with Safiya: his blue eyes carried this good man watermark. His whole demeanor carried a good man DNA. He had that eager and will-ing-to-please look. I thought that maybe I should just point him in the right direction.

I talked to a good friend of mine who was seduced in his early twenties by a woman in her mid thirties. They actually are still married. He habitually cheats to complement his life, but he still finds his wife doable at the age of fifty. I thought that since I do not believe in forever anyway, it does not really matter. When Muslims break the fast, they usually eat a big feast. Young Tim had the right ingredients for a big feast to satisfy a sex-dehydrated woman. I tried to justify the fantasy for myself. I thought, well I am now a veteran of love. I should just share my war experience with young Tim.

I decided not to pursue young Tim. He can just read my book and learn everything about my experiences. It is fun to drive by the maternity ward and look at the young hope. It is fun to fantasize about gang robbing the cradle with my friend Safiya. I do have the ideal size boobs for breastfeeding and I did want to pick up the young Tim and nurse him. However, I am not a cradle robber. I will follow my fast. Maybe in September, I will join the big manhunt season to secure a boyfriend for the holidays. Maybe I will sit out this coming season; good players deserve a break. Maybe I will find an older lover. Maybe I will find a young lover, but 1980 has to be my cut-off year. That way the young lover would qualify for a mighty meal.

Afterword:

Now almost two years after the happy meal story that started my interest in younger partners, my only criticism is that American culture still assigns almost a sexless role for women in their forties and fifties. Intergeneration love is only accepted for males seeking young women. It should be accepted in both directions. Having sexual interest in younger partners is natural. Women are called cougars, while men brag about their younger partners. We have to make a cultural shift accepting women seeking younger partners without fear of reprisal. We have to do it and rather quickly. It is urgent as I am turning forty soon. Of course, once we break the old stereotypes, new ones will rise.

Reactions to the first edition:

I knew that the book would have enemies, but some of the critics came from close friends. A doctor friend said, "Your book has no intrinsic value." That was harsh, but he is a loveable geek so I did not take it personally. Another friend asked how I could consider my book spiritual. I had to walk him through it. I asked him if sex was a carnal experience only. He answered immediately that sex is a body and soul experience. Then I asked him why he could not consider a book about sex spiritual. He sat there quietly and changed the topic.

Frequently asked questions:

I wrote that the story of my rebound guy was not included in this first edition of the book out of deference and that I owed a cosmic debt for sending him into my life. Today, I happily report that I paid my cosmic debt by being there for Paul from sexual pilgrimage, as he was recently divorced. That sentence triggered a lot of questions from readers. Some readers insisted that I should have included the story. Some readers asked if I did not respect my other partners. Let me tell you what my rebound guy did for me. He brought me a mirror and asked me to look at myself and admire my body. He said, "Today my love, you are the centerfold." He introduced me to my clitoris. He said, "Samara, meet your best friend." He bought me a vibrator to break the ice the first time I met my clitoris. He asked me to touch myself. He guided my hand and watched me. He took a divorced woman with broken self-esteem and did major reconstruction. We could not stay with each others for reasons which we could not control. At the airport, as we parted, we went to the restroom and had our final goodbye sex.

Miscellaneous questions from interviews:

1) Why did you write, *When the Veil Drops?*

I wanted my experiences to be filtered through the prism of each reader. I believe that raising the nature of consciousness through an introspective book is a central part of contemporary feminism.

2) Would you ever sleep with one of your girlfriend's husbands?

The answer is hell no. I know how bad they are.

3) Why do you like married men?

I confess that I like married men a little more than I like single men. It is like a product that got highly recommended and the ring is a seal of approval. Sometimes my sexual preferences express themselves in triangular configuration. I call it my love pyramid. I guess that it adds textual layering, which brings intrigue to the love story.

4) Did you ever think about suing the doctor from *sharmoota?*

No, the sex was good.

5) Did anyone in your family practice polygamy?

Yes, my aunt was a second wife. She was pretty and younger than the first one. The first wife picked her because she knew her husband would have to treat both of them equally. With a pretty young second wife, she knew their husband would bring them gifts and jewelry equally. Basically, she wanted to have a bad husband part-time, receive some gifts, and not lose any of her status.

6) Which is better — an affair or a second marriage?

With an affair the other woman sees the good side of your husband. When he is with her, he is exciting and living the dream. With a second wife, she shares the good and bad side of the husband.

7) Do you believe that all men who refuse to cheat are losers?
The only exception to this rule is a military man, because
if he withheld from having affairs, the reason is a male
reason — "his career."

8) As a Muslim, how did you allow yourself to have back door
action?
I followed verse 223 from chapter 2, Al Baqarah, from the
Koran: "Your women are a place of cultivation so come to
your place however you wish." This question came from a
female Muslim friend and reader of my book. Her husband
evidently really wanted some back door action. One time he
threatened to divorce her and she still denied him, fearing
God. I explained to her that to deny the husband is a sin
and that however her husband wants her, she should obey.
I actually gave her a good lube and told her have fun.

9) Do you agree with Freudian insistence on the centrality of
the phallus in the unconscious?
Yes, I do. In fact, I constantly wear a long pendant when I
have on a low-cut dress. In a way, I like having a phallic sym-
bol between my boobs. Also, having a long pendant allows
men to compliment me on something when I catch them
staring.

10) What was your harshest critic?
A self-declared feminist said that she would have liked the
book if I did not include "vulgarities." I do not agree with
her and I do not see why I should be censored in the land
of the free. I found myself thinking of what would have happened to American sexual culture if the writing of Simone
de Beauvoir had been translated word for word. She had
an amazing influence on early feminists. Would they have
rejected her writing if the word "*Baiser*" was translated cor-
rectly into its equivalent fuck?

Questions from friends:
I received a question from a man whom I pleasured orally. He
wondered why he was not included in the book. I consider oral sex
just a display of good manners. I was perfecting my technique and
he received an incidental benefit. Now, you are included in the
second edition, my friend.

I did not expect it, but the one partner who was not mentioned felt left out. It was not by design; I just did not write his story.

Some readers bought used copies with an interesting dedication. Yes, I wrote few dedications to Bill Maher. He is my absolute favorite comedian, so I pretended that he read and enjoyed a personal copy. Sometimes, I wrote sarcastic dedications. For instance to the man I found the least attractive, I wrote, "I find you handsome," "I found you sexy." When I gave the book to the man who exudes magnetic sexual power and represents my ultimate crush, I did not write a dedication to the one who can have me at any time and anywhere. He has a copy without a dedication.

Second edition, new story

Lunch-time wife
Monday May 18, 2010

My nipples salute him as he passes me in the hallway.

"Congratulations, Samara. I read your book. I see that I did not make it there," Lieutenant McGregor said jokingly. My book *When the Veil Drops* is a personal memoir where I showered naked over the pages of the book. I pulled a Saint Augustine confessions-style book, without the redemption.

"Of course you did. It is the unpublished story," I answered playfully.

He laughed and we got interrupted again. Every conversation between us is a stillborn child robbed of its happy life. Sometimes he has a chance of saying one word: "later." I fell in love with his "later" promises.

Tuesday May 19, 2010

I ran into Lieutenant McGregor at the gym today. Chief Laura saw me looking at him. She stopped me at the women's locker room. "Hey Samara, I saw you looking at LT today; give the guy a fighting chance," she said as she was stepping into the shower. I smiled at her comment. I told Laura that somehow when I think of LT and myself getting sweaty together, the picture did not include two parallel treadmills. Laura laughed. She said, "You are not an Arabic teacher. You were hired to hijack American men, one married man at a time."

LT has a presence which enslaves me. He activates my dormant Arabic subservient women's genes. I imagine myself taking off his shoes, washing his feet in lukewarm water, and massaging his feet. I imagine myself becoming his *Misyar* wife or lunch-time wife. It is an Islamic practice called *Misyar*. It is a common practice in Gulf countries. Initially this practice started if a Muslim was on travel or away from home and still wanted sex. Now, it is still used especially for *Thayeb* (divorced women) who have no chance in landing single men for husbands. Once a woman loses her virginity in a first marriage she is considered used goods. All return goods must go half price. Unlike the regular second wife who has the right to equal time as the first wife, a *Misyar* wife can only see her husband during lunch time or during his travel.

Wednesday May 20, 2010

Today, I ran into LT in the break room. He took one look at my feta cheese salad and said, "What are you eating? That does not look good." He offered me his white looking sausage. "I don't eat meat." I answered him politely. He looked at me with penetrating eyes. His eyes said that he knew my lips could suck a juicy leg of lamb dry. He was right. I have sucked my fair share of succulent legs of lamb.

"I am just watching what I eat, so no meat for me," I replied.

"Nonsense! You will be having my sausage today. Plus, Samara, it is Trader's Joe's famous seafood sausage," LT said in his powerful commanding voice.

I ate his sausage. I insisted on washing the plate. I told him that men were not supposed to wash dishes. He turned a little red. He did an about face and left the break room. I went to the bathroom to change my always pad. I was on overdrive.

Thursday May 21, 2010

I decided that I was not going to wait for LT to make a move. I decided to call him.

He answered his phone: "Unit … LT … non secure line. Can I help you, sir … ma'am?"

I wanted to ask for a secure line to launch my attack on him. I answered him trying to milk my French accent, "Yes, as matter of fact you can. Can we have lunch sometime?"

"We do have lunch sometimes. We had lunch yesterday," Lt. answered with a smile I could see on the phone.

"I don't want to have lunch in the break room."

"Where do you want to have lunch?"

"I want to have lunch in my house," I announced firmly.

"You want to have lunch in your house," he repeated in disbelief.

"Yes, my house. I live close. I can cook for you."

"Pick a place, any place, and we can have lunch next Wednesday."

"I picked a place and you did not like it. You pick a place and email me."

He said Wednesday, hump day; was that a good sign? I wondered.

Friday May 22, 2010

Friday is always a good day at work. I was leaving early that Friday. Then I ran into LT on the stairs. "Look at you!" said LT.

I smiled. "Are all your sentences orders, sir?"

"Hey, are all your sentences questions? Women of all colors love their interrogatives. I know how to talk to Arab women and for you I use imperatives. Now tell me, where you going looking like that?"

"Today is the last day of the opera season; I am going to see Madame Butterfly."

"Wow, you like opera. I always knew that you're my Glenn Close," said Lt.

When friends use a colloquial expression, I get this blank stare which denotes a small cultural pothole. My exotic eyes look dumb when I have these blank stares. He noticed and explained. He said, "Samara, now you have your orders. Watch *Fatal Attraction* and have a good weekend."

I knew that I had to obey. That weekend my determination drove me all over town to find the movie. Other than the curly hair, I had nothing in common with Glenn Close. I hated that movie. How did a successful woman turn into an obsessed freaking rabbit killer?

On Monday, I got a phone message with the name of the restaurant. On Tuesday I was writing all kind of rated R scenarios for our first lunch.

Wednesday May 27, 2010

I had to go to lunch ten minutes late. I called him to apologize. He said that he was going to order food for me. I loved that. He was sitting with another man from a different office. I thought that was not the kind of ménage a trois I liked. He introduced me to Bill. He said that he owed both of us lunches so he decided to treat us at the same time. I got the message. My dream officer turned out to be an officer and a gentleman. I stopped running into LT but I still look at his hallway picture.

Part Two

My Islam

I accept that Muslim readers may hate my book, but I do not accept if they question my religion. One of my female readers tried to get a Muslim Imam (Islamic leader) to read my book. He refused adamantly and told her that, "The writer of such a book can't be Muslim." She was trying to start a healthy discussion and ask questions that she could not ask directly. When he refused to read the book, he closed the door on that honest discussion. She told me that she was disappointed because he acted very "progressive," yet he refused to read the book. I was not surprised. To him I say, "More men converted to Islam for me than you, dear Imam."

To those who asked how am I still considered Muslim, I need to remind them of An-Nisa Chapter 4, verse 48:

"Indeed, Allah does not forgive association with Him, but he forgives what is less than that for whom He wills. And he who associates others with Allah has certainly fabricated a tremendous sin."

The same verse is almost repeated in verse 116; who has the right to denounce another Muslim? The answer is no one has this right. Allah the merciful God can and will forgive mistakes other than worshiping others. Allah is the judge and I am not accepting other judges.

My Islam is an English translation of my Islamic conviction. My Islam is the Islam for Allah and his prophet, not the Islam of *Fiqh* (interpretation of Islamic principles) and the scholars. I practice my own *Ijtihad* (Interpretation of Islam). I believe it was Jasper who said, "All knowledge is interpretation." I do my own interpretation. I spend more time seeking my own truth. God prefers those who seek the truth and do not follow blindly. Let's read this verse from Al-Furqan, chapter 25, verse 73:

"And those who, when reminded of the verses of their Lord, do not fall upon them deaf and blind."

I understand why some people would follow blindly. It is unavoidable byproduct of illiteracy but why would intellectuals do the same? I believe that Islamic practices and the established knowledge provide a fertile ground to grow terrorism. We moderate Muslims are leaving a wide gap. We need to examine our views and realize what beliefs are socially constructed beliefs and which comes from Islam. We need to ask if there is evidence in support of the claims. Sometimes, I am sure that we can find a slight modification of a claim which would eliminate potential logical inconsistency.

Let me give you an example instead of talking in general. I do not believe that stoning is lawful in Islam. Some of the explanation provided by scholars satisfies the emotional needs of jealous husbands, but has no roots in Islam. I do not think the prophet stoned Aisha when her reputation came into question. Aisha stayed in with her parents' house for one month before the verse which proved her innocence came to the prophet. I do not think that her father rushed to kill her for honor either. Stoning became a punishment for adultery under the misogynist Omar (Second caliphate).

Let's read An-Nisa chapter 4, verse 15:

"Those who commit unlawful sexual intercourse of your women, bring against four witnesses from among you and if they testify, confine them to houses until death takes them or Allah ordains for them another way."

So even with the testimony of four witnesses, God said to keep them secluded in their house and did not say stone them to death. Let's read further the following verse:

"And the two who commit it among you punish them both. But if they repent and correct themselves, leave them alone. Indeed, Allah is ever accepting of repentance and Merciful."

Please note the use of the dual form used in here, the punishment is not only for women, but for the two partners. Even the word punish could be interpreted as dishonor. There is no mention of stoning them. In fact the punishment can't be stoning because it takes away their chance to repent. If we put it in layman terms — oh, I like that expression — maybe because it has lay and man in one word. I am easily distracted. What was I saying again? Ah, I remember now. Stoning can't be the punishment as it precludes the chance for repentance.

Muslims lie with *Hadith* (Prophet speeches and sayings), the way Westerners lie with statistics. You know what I mean. Chances are you have been in a discussion and made up a statistic to confirm your argument. Well, Muslims would bring up a *Hadith* and say the prophet said such and such. I had a friend who always said, "There is a *Hadith* for that," in the same way my thirteen-year-old boy say there is an "app" for that.

Muslims pick and choose the *Hadith* suitable for their conversations and denounce the others as *Hadith* which were made up by … yes, you guessed it, the Jews. There is no virtually nothing wrong that is not blamed on the Jews. So the story goes that during the *Hadith*, the prophet was asked about a woman's Jihad and the prophet said that a woman's Jihad is her obedience to her husband. Why would I buy this *Hadith*?

The prophet himself allowed women to participate in battles and not just as nurses. The name of Nusaybah Bint Kaab and her brave role in the battle of *Uhud* comes to mind. Why would the prophet limit women's role to mere obedience?

Let me give you another example of a current Islamic belief which I reject. It is kind of a big one. Are you ready? I do not accept the Islamic claim to Jerusalem. The claim is based on the fact that God ordained prayers during the miraculous trip of the prophet to Jerusalem. I believe that *Qiblah* (the direction where Muslims pray) is more important criteria. The prophet prayed toward Jerusalem until a verse from God changed the direction to Mecca. Let's read Al- Baqara, chapter 2, verse 144:

"We have certainly seen the turning of your face, and we will surely turn you to a qiblah with which you will be pleased. So turn your face toward Al-Masjid Al-Haram. And wherever you believers are turn your faces toward it. Indeed, those who have been given the Scripture well know that it is the truth from their Lord. And Allah is not unaware of what they do."

As the verse explained, God knew that the prophet's preference was Jerusalem, but God ordered him toward Mecca and promised that it was the better choice for Muslims. Why do we Muslims seem to accept God's will as the one size fits all answer to everything except for Jerusalem?

I am troubled with the inconsistency of claims of Islamic practices with Koran. I spend a lot of my time reading the Koran and books, analyzing the internal validity of these claims, and looking for sound and cogent arguments while rejecting weak ones.

I would need another book just to discuss my research in Koran, *Hadith,* and Islamic books of *Fiqh.*

In summary, I am a practicing Muslim, but what I practice is my Islam.

7 Myths about Muslims

As we say in Arabic, there is no smoke without a fire. Some of these myths are only partially true and some are complete fabricated fiction. A close friend suggested that I address each of them:

Myth#1: Muslim women are treated equal to men under Islamic laws.

It is true that Islam put the same responsibilities on women, but did it give them the same rights? Dr. Fatima Naja in her book, *Westerners and the Muslim woman*, talks about the great achievement Islam made for women. For example, it fought infanticide. Islam regulated marriages, divorce, and put a limit on polygamy. It gave women the right to inherit and have separate financial accounts. She even viewed the fact that Koran removed the guilt of the original sin from Eve as giving women more power. Yes, God put a limit of four wives in verse 3 of chapter 4, with the stipulation of treating them equally. However, in verse 129 of the same chapter God said, "And you will never be able to be equal between wives even if you should strive to do so." My dear readers, you know that I personally like polygamy. However, it is just an example of how scholars ignore interpreting what pleases them. In fact, some translation of Koran, realizing that the later verse would negate the earlier one, adds the words "equal in feeling." In Arabic, the words "in feeling" is not specified.

Dr. Fatima Naja warns Muslim women that westerners want to drag them to the workforce. She praises Islam for making men responsible for paying for the women, but she misses the point that with spending money comes the complete control over women as stipulated by verse 34 of chapter 4. "Men are in charge of women by right of what Allah has given them and what they spend from their wealth."

Myth # 2: All Muslim women keep their virginity before marriage.

As far as generalization goes, this is a good one. There are some good Muslim girls raised to stay virgins until married. The magic formula is a mixture of fear of God and fear of getting killed, since honor killing is a prevalent practice in Muslim communities.

There are sad cases of honor killing where the victims were killed because their fathers or brothers suspected that they lost their virginity. Of course for me the sad part is that these victims did not get any sex before they died.

There are other Muslim girls raised under the same conditions, but they seek comfort in other girls and engage in same-sex relationships until married. Some of them stop and some continue to have these relationships even after their marriages. They just have to learn to conceal them. I traveled to Jordan in 2008 for a conference. I went to an all women hairdresser to get my hair done. The shop offered several services. I asked for the Brazilian wax which was only $12. Then Sumayah, who was a nice Iraqi woman in her late twenties, asked me if I wanted the full service for only $20. I told her that it was not necessary thinking that she meant waxing my legs. She was very hesitant to explain it. She started by saying the application of "cooling gel." Then eventually she said that she meant an "oil change." That expression is a code word in Arabic culture for sex. Now she had my attention.

I paid her that $20 just to talk to her. She explained to me that rich Iraqi left early before the war. They started businesses in Jordan but the local hated the influx of Iraqis who came with money. Then the second wave of Iraqis came and they were the poor ones who fled after the war. Jordanians do not pay the poor Iraqi workers full wages. Some of the Iraqi women worked as prostitutes for men. Others worked in women's shops as prostitutes for women. I could not understand Sumayah's logic, but somehow offering services for women was more honorable. I talked to all the Iraqi workers in the shop that day and asked about their female customers, who all wear the veil and most are married. I paid each of them the $20 to talk to me and no, I did not get my oil changed that day. It turns out that the all-female hairdresser was offering all kinds of services for customers.

There are other Muslims girls who have the means to cheat the system as there is an illegal surgery to fix the hymen. It is typically done in after-hours clinics by nurses. I am not sure how it is done. I was told that it can't be done to circumcised girls. I guess that is why they still circumcise women. There is a Chinese product now called "virgin in a bag," which is similar to Halloween fake blood. I was tempted to purchase one just to inspect it, but then again, my virginity — as you well know — is ancient history.

Myth #3: It is easy for Muslim women to get a divorce.

I have heard this argument from a number of American women when discussing Muslim women. Their argument is always the same. They think that if Muslim women really hated the way their husbands treated them, they would definitely get a divorce. Here is a little trivia for you; in Pashto, the word ex-wife does not exist. Afghan culture does not allow divorce.

If we reverse the myth and say it is easy for Muslim men to get a divorce, the sentence would be a true statement. Muslim men can easily divorce their wives. In fact, all the man has to do is to say, "I divorce you." If the woman is lucky, he will repeat it three times and that is a final divorce. If a Muslim man divorces his wife once he still has the option to return her within three months.

Unless the marriage contract stipulates that the wife can divorce her husband, a clause called *Esma,* it is very hard for Muslim women to seek a divorce. There is a rather recent practice in Egypt based on an old Islamic practice called *Khulaa.* It allows Egyptian women to seek dissolution of the marriage; however, the wife has to give up all her rights of financial support.

Myth# 4: Temporary marriages are illegal in Islam.

First a definition is needed. Yes, if you specify a period on the marriage contract, it invalidates it. However, if you do not put the duration you can be married for twenty minutes or months or years. There are four variations of temporary marriages: *Mutah, Urfee, Sighah,* and *Misyar. Mutah* is the Arabic word for pleasure. Again if you do not specify the duration then the contract is legal. All you need are two male witnesses and a piece of paper. The main difference is the woman enters the contract by herself and none of her family members give her away. *Urfee* is the secret kind of temporary marriages. Well, all temporary marriages could be kept secret, but *Urfee* is typically a secret as it is more common among young generations. They are using *Urfee* marriages to facilitate their union without the involvement of parents. The rising costs associated with marriages means it is not easy to be able to afford the wedding, the apartment, the furniture, and yes, the dowry, which all fall on the groom.

Sighah is the Farsi word for temporary marriage and it is the registered type of temporary marriage in Iran. *Misyar* is a temporary marriage based on convenience. For instance, if you become a geographical bachelor, you are allowed to have another wife in your new location. This type of marriage is perfect for widows and divorced women, especially those who have children. I was offered a *Misyar* marriage upon my divorce. As a divorced woman, I am considered used goods and I had to go half price. Shihab was a wealthy man from UAE. He offered to take his three hours lunch nap in my place. He was very generous in his offer of accommodations, car, driver, school for my son, and "stipend." He made sure to say that he gave me an offer he would not give a Moroccan woman. That is a compliment, by the way; Moroccan women are known to be … hmm, how should I put it … the more sexually active. I liked him but not sufficiently to leave my country and move to Dubai for an afternoon delight. I still think about how different my life would have been if I moved to UAE and became Shihab's Moroccan.

Myth #5: A Muslim husband can't punish his wife.

Islam allows a Muslim man to punish his wife in three different ways as detailed in chapter 4 An-Nisa, verse 34: "Men are in charge of women by right of what Allah has given one over the other and what they spend from their wealth. So righteous women are devoutly obedient, guarding in their husband's absence what Allah would have them guard. But those wives from whom you fear arrogance advise them; then forsake them in bed; and strike them. But if they obey you seek no means against them. Indeed, Allah is ever exalted and Grand." I have known a lot of Muslim men who practice their rights of hitting their wives. The nice ones would hit gently. Some give what I call "reminder" hitting regularly to their wives. Like most battered women, they side with their husbands, but in the Muslim women's case, women feel that their husbands are justified.

Myth # 6: There are no gays in Muslim countries.

We owe this funny joke of a myth to Mahmoud Ahmadinejad, president of Iran. Okay Mahmoud, so no one was interested in you, but that does not mean there are no gays. You remind me of an ugly woman who went to the bar and no one was interested, so she left the bar thinking it was a gay bar. I addressed the topic of homosexuality in a different section, but I had to list it in the myth section as well. I am very supportive of gay men; of course, what unites us is the love of an erect penis.

Myth# 7: God does not see what happens on an island

If you visit Bahrain, you hear this myth repeated over and over. Bahrain is sin island for Saudis. You might even see Saudis flicking a drop of their drinks before they drink them. You might hear them say it is because the prophet (May peace be upon him) said to Muslims not to let the first drop of alcohol touch your lips. All these are lies and jokes developed by Saudis. God's omnipresence is central to Islamic belief.

My take on wearing the veil "Hijab"

I personally do not believe that wearing the *hijab* is mandated by Islam for all Muslim women. In the early days of Islam, all free women wore a head covering except for the slaves. Since *Hijab* was a way of identifying slaves from free women, it should have been abolished at the same time slavery was abolished. The reason is given in Al-Ahazb chapter 33, verse 59:

"O prophet, tell your wives and your daughters and the women of the believers to bring down over themselves of their outer garments. That is more suitable that they will be known and not be abused. And ever is Allah Forgiving and Merciful."

Additionally following the same reasoning of protection of women, Muslim women who live in non-Muslim countries should not wear the *Hijab* because there is a potential of abuse if they are identified as Muslims.

Let's read the verse used by scholars to make the veil mandatory. An-Noor chapter 24, verse 31:

"And tell the believing women to lower their gaze and guard their private parts and not expose their adornment except which appears from it and wrap their head covers over their pockets not to expose their adornment except to their husbands ..."

The translation of this previous verse adds the word "necessarily appears" and substitutes the word pockets with chests. I believe this translation not to be an accurate meaning in Arabic. First the expression "except which appears from it" refers to the face and hands, which the prophet explains in one of the *Hadith*. There is proof to say that the face and hands should not be covered. Why are scholars choosing to ignore it? *Niqab*, which means to cover the face, is unlawful and there is no proof that early Muslim women ever wore it. I fully support a ban on *Niqab*. It is a huge security risk because you can't tell who is behind the *Niqab*. It is what the prophet called *Bedaah* (something made up) and every *Bedaah* is unlawful in Islam.

Second, we do not know about the old Arabic garment. Maybe the pockets were located at the upper arms or lower at the hips. How can we say that we know for sure that pockets were located at the chest area? Again, the whole point was to differentiate between Muslim women and non-Muslim women of *Jahiliat*. However, since we do not have pictures or specific details, it does not matter.

To ban wearing the *Hijab* is not a liberating solution. We have a recent example in modern history. In 1935, Reza Shah in Iran put a ban on women wearing the *Shador* (Persian version of Hijab). Men forced their daughters to stop going to school and women were sequestered. Muslim women have to decide for themselves. Two years ago, I had the idea of doing a qualitative study on the experience of American Muslim women wearing the *Hijab* in the American education system. I was two chapters in when I decided to abandon my dissertation. Some of my close friends advised me to finish it; after all, a dissertation is only five chapters. I had to abandon it because I had expectations based on my personal belief, which turned out to be wrong. I took a year break from school. It was a forced break, as I was academically disqualified. However, I had to reflect on my work and I realized that I did not do well on that topic because it was emotionally all consuming to me. I thought that most women were forced to wear *Hijab* by their male family members: fathers, brothers, and husbands. That was simply not the case for the women I interviewed.

I divided the women into three age categories: under twenty-one, twenty-one to twenty-eight and twenty-nine to thirty-five. I interviewed seven in each category. Since interviews were conducted under the guise of study and not for the purpose of a book, I will not name the participants.

The theme that emerged in the younger age category was sexual intrigue. "I get fewer headaches from my father and *Hijab* draws more men to me," said a nineteen-year-old woman. "I am more erotic while I do not have to deal with my kinky hair," said another nineteen-year-old. I thought, well, I have curly hair as well, but my cure was a flat iron. "Americans find me attractive and seductive," said an eighteen-year-old, laughing. She added, "They think that I will do the seven veils dance for them or that I come with a harem of women."

As I interviewed these young women, I noticed how they color-coordinated their scarves with their clothing. In many cases, they wore fitted clothing and looked at the scarf like an accessory. I think that wearing *Hijab* in western countries is counterintuitive. The whole idea behind *Hijab* is to stop the wandering eyes of men. My best American Christian friend Safiya is more modest than any of these young women. She has a size six sexy body and constantly wears dowdy clothing. I tease her, saying that she has a self-imposed "invisible burka." She would never wear neck-plunging blouses and show off her double D-sized boobs. I gave her a friendly massage the other day and I got a little excited: her knockers are simply majestic. Back to our topic, before I get distracted. Wearing *Hijab* in western countries make women stand out and invites the wandering eyes. I call on Muslim scholars. We need a fatwa, making wearing *Hijab* in Western countries *Haram/*unlawful.

One of the themes that dominated the interviews in the two older categories was the sense of liberation. They saw the *Hijab* as their line of defense against western cultures, which objectified women. "Wearing the *Hijab* forces men to look me in the eye and treat me like equal," said a thirty-year-old woman. I struggled with that notion and the term "Islamic uniform" kept repeating in my mind. I started to question my personal motives. I wanted to be my idol, a new age Huda Sharawi, but quickly found out that women will not line up after me. It is hard to liberate those who do not see the shackles.

I support all Muslims women who want to stop the practice of wearing *Hijab* as much as I support those women who want to wear it. Sadly, I have to acknowledge that it has become part of a social identifier and part of the identity of Muslim women.

My take on homosexuality in Arab countries

~

Arab teachers would say, "Arab countries have no gays and that expression is a vicious rumor started by the Jews." I laughed so hard one time that the Saudi teacher in class asked me to leave the room. For most Arabs, Jews are the bogeyman and the source of all evil and aberration, but that is another topic.

In my opinion, societies where contact with the opposite sex is forbidden might as well institutionalize homosexuality. In a culture where the husband humiliates and disparages the wife in front of the children and only maleness is celebrated breeds homoerotic tendencies. Women have to seek empathy within women and men are drinking the elixir of their superiority at early stages of development.

Let's inspect the word for gay in Arabic — "*Manyouk.*" It only means the receiver. So in a way, you are only considered gay if you are on the receiving end of the transaction. In Iraqi, the word is "Farkh," which means little chick denoting a tendency to liking prepubescent boys.

I do not want you to think that when you see men holding hands in Arab countries that they are all gay. Holding hands is a sign of friendship. In fact, if there is any kind of gay relationship between two people, you will find them displaying public hostility to safeguard their secret.

There were men lovers in the time of early Islam as evidenced by chapter 26, verse 164: "And leave what your Lord has created for you as mates? But you are a people transgressing."

Gays in Koran are referred to as people of Lot, and the word for a gay person is *Lootee.*

It is time for Muslim gays to come out of their deep, very deep closets and for Islam to accept them. We keep saying that Islam is the most tolerant religion.Why don't we show it by embracing Muslims of all sexual orientations?

In Koran, God punished the people of Lot (gays) by heavy rain. If we as Muslims claim that our religion is the religion of tolerance, then we should show some tolerance and accept all Muslims. My hope is for the surviving gays to see the rainbow at the end of the rain.

My take on marriage

I disagree with the term sex addict. If sex is a substance needed for life, then you can't say he or she is addicted to sex. It is like saying he is addicted to water. I was called a sex addict by some of my partners. When I told my friends that I would fast, they laughed. I started the fast on March 8, 2010. Sure, I felt itches that I could not scratch but I did it.

In the American society, we live in the matrix of monogamy and every husband who cheats has to go to sex rehab or risk having his privileges cancelled. What the society calls sex addiction, I call natural urges. When marriages were invented, humans lived to be — what — thirty-years-old? I believe that marriage contracts should be renewable every three, five, or seven years. You can choose whichever period of performance suits you and your partner best. Then when the time is up both of you can decide to either renew it or exchange goodbye gifts.

To enter into a legal contract with a permanent mating partner is irrational. To think that you will be able to recreate the same stimulus situations or that you will have the same sexual drives over the years is simply not practical. To build a lasting social construct built on sex is illogical. What ties partners together should be social, not sexual, in nature. I should be allowed to marry my best female friend. We think alike. We finish each other sentences. We have what it takes to have a lasting relationship. We can support each other financially and emotionally. Who we sleep with together or separately should be just our business. It is irrelevant.

Erotic excitement and concluding remarks

I believe that our personal myths, beliefs, and early memories write the script of our fantasies. I highly recommend that each reader go back to every daydream and discover his or her untold story. Initially, I just wanted to share my candid story and have each reader extrapolate his or her own story from my observations. I wanted to define my sexual index and place my sexuality into that collective unconscious pool. I needed to go beyond facts, feelings, and names. It is very liberating to learn the inner meaning of our raw desires. I am aware that it is a little dangerous as well. Some mysteries are meant to stay mysteries.

My true erotic perversion is exhibitionism. A man can be arrested for exhibiting his genitals. As a woman my true crime is exhibiting my inner thoughts. By taking a snapshot of my memories and analyzing them, I wanted to free myself of the limits of personal history of relationships. Sexual choreography is my passion. I love to see partners dance.

Here is what I learned about myself after I analyzed every sexual fantasy and every sexual encounter. I understood how I always wrote each sexual script, cast the actor, and mounted the production. I looked back on how I helped an unidentified gay man and moved him into the confirmed gay category. My strong animus usually attracts unidentified gay men and now I am aware of it. Power was the common denominator in all my sexual scripts, either power which I seek to absorb or power which I seek to transmit. I realized that I only liked tall men because I equated being tall with a sense of power. When a short man displayed the same power, I made what I thought was the exception and pursued a short man. However in reality, I was still after that raw power of masculinity.

Freud talked about the repetition compulsion. After I analyzed and understood the personal dynamics of my erotic excitement, I freed myself from the need to replay and repeat. Maybe I made myself less beddable in the process, but at least I reached my goal of clarity.

Today, I proudly announce that I played all the sex roles I need. I was the wife. The experience was similar to giving a Mercedes to a student driver. To be fair, though, he was a well-endowed student driver. I was the concubine. I played the slave who served her master; even that role was exhilarating in small doses. I had my fair share of temporary marriages.

Today, I know my sexual index and here are some of my preferences. I like women, but only as a side dish. Their sensitivity entices me, but their possessiveness turns me off. I like the older man because his advances are gentle and unhurried. I like the young man because of that sexual urgency he displays. I confess sometimes I want a human baboon who is going to be dominant. He will decide when to take me. Sometimes I want a human chimpanzee who is going to be cruel and unkind. I prefer a hyper-sexed male monkey, who goes from a tree to another to copulate, to an eagle who mates for life.

Today, at the age of thirty-eight, my breeding days are behind me. I should prefer the herd to the male. However, after months of self-imposed no sex diet, my pussy turned into an octopus suction cup and it should come with a warning of possible desintegration of any object inserted. I still wake up craving a cup of semen every morning. I am sure that sometime soon I will give out my willingness signals and engage in the temporary mating ritual again.

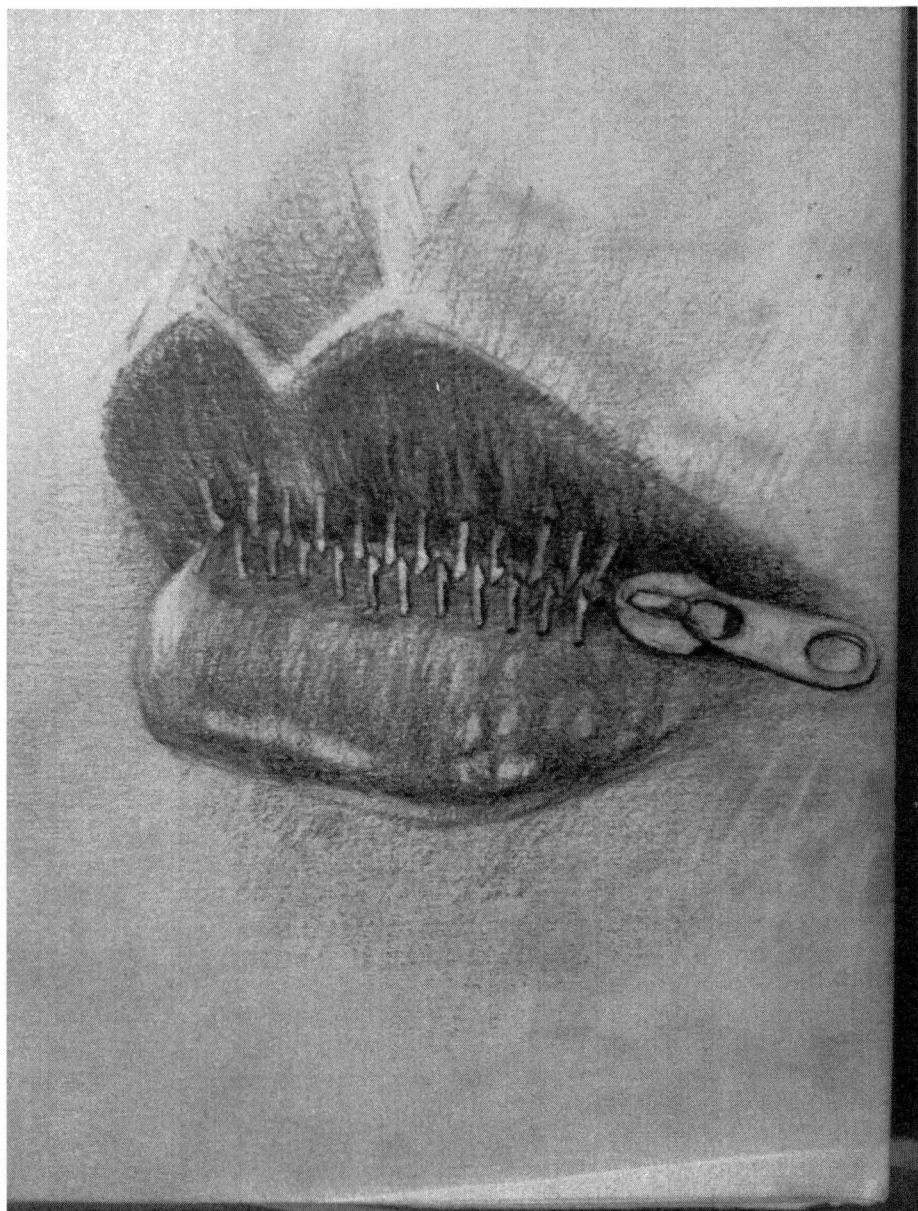

Part Three

❧

"I saw your daring eyes
Looking through the hole in the wall
It pierced a hole in me
It made an exhibitionist out of me
Suddenly, I wanted you to see
To see me to feel me
I am promised to a cousin
He does not see
He never looked at me
My father was right
Girls should never learn
How to write"
Lunday: Poetry published anonymously and
written by Afghan women.

Before I share the translation of my Arabic poems, here is the first poem I wrote in English. I wrote it to my officer and gentleman from lunch-time wife:

Lust, lust, lust
An unbearable lust
A domesticated dick, I crave
Oh, my heart be brave!
Seamless ambiguity,
Sure uncertainty
Infantile drive
A sigh of relief
Consciously deny me
Unconsciously take me
Blur your awareness
Bring your senses
We only sin when we know
Why not let ourselves go?

Translation
Poem 1
O my Arab bird
Fly into the sky of my desire
I control the rainfall
Heavy or light showers
Drop, drop
Rituals to Fuck with me
Codes to love me
I will teach you all the symbols
I will decide who wins
O my Arabic horse
Run in the circle of my desire
Quickly or slowly
Stop, stop
I will give you the directions
I'll give you directions
I'll plan your moves
Do you recognize me?
Let me introduce myself

I'm the horse rider

Poem 2
On the wedding day
As a gift for pureness and honor
My mother gave me advice
She spoke frankly
Your fragility is your strength
Your tears are your ammunition
Women, all women are Amina
And Amina pleases her husband
Be a female, be Amina
The tears of her humiliation wrote the lines
I listened in disbelief
I cried the weakness of my mother and my psychological inheritance
I announced my independence and my refusal of a stupid destiny

Note:
Amina is a character known to be Mrs. Obedient in one of an Egyptian Writer, Naguib Mahfouz.

Poem 3
Sex is my prayer
Your eyes undress me
Your whispers play with my shyness
Your smell touches my body
Your kisses purify my heart
Your fingers play with m y pussy
You free me of all my chains
You erase my sins
You submerge me with life
When you enter me

Poem 4
I came to you stripped of words
My love, I'm not that good in the art of maneuvering

My eyes do not transmit signals
My body sends messages
Tear it, read it
Don't stand in front of me confused
Wasting my time is a major sin
You desire me, I desire you
You crave me, I crave you
I don't care who starts
It doesn't matter what people say

Poem 5

Eve: "Adam, my life, accept my apology."
Adam: "My love, don't leave me behind!"
Eve: "I sinned, Satan made me slip."
Adam: "No, he made us slip."
Eve: "I'll go away."
Adam: "Don't leave heaven. It is hell without you."
Eve: "You will live damned with me."
Adam: "I'll be crazy without you."
Eve: "I'm scared."
Adam: "Our love is the guidance."
Eve: "And earth?"
Adam: "Our way out is the beginning."

Poem 6

In this poem, the writer put a new twist on an old folktale of
Laila and Qais. Qais was a poet who wrote about his beloved
Laila. Her family did not allow him to marry her because of his
poetry. In this poem he talks about Laila's point of view who
refused to marry Qais.
Oh Qais
Be depressed all your life because of our separation
Write whatever you want in my eyes
I wasn't searching for a kind heart
I wanted a teacher of sensuality
Oh Qais, you are well known for your daring attitude
I met you alone
I discovered you to be man of words

And I, my love
Don't like poetry or words
I chose another man
He is not a poet
But his pen is powerful
He doesn't read or write
But he writes verses inside me
Tales are told about these verses

Poem 7
A poem or narrative
Poetry or thoughts
Rhymes or grammar
My words are brand new
Words made of slaves' tears
I'm not writing a poem
Enough with the poems
I'm not listing a thought
Enough with the thoughts
My words rebelled against all the tears
My words refused shyness
My friend, don't weigh my words
My words are heavy with sorrow
Words are not to be read
But
Felt by the innocent

Poem 8
My body became like a cobweb
And who knows what a cobweb is
The weakest one is the cobweb
I have a dream
I see you caught in the web
I see you dying happily
They said that he is a victim
I said he is a martyr
His beloved one is a female spider

Poem 9

I was born a female
A name preceded by a preposition
A name meant to be an indirect object
He was born a man
A name meant to be a subject
A name that doesn't know oppression
I untie all the nodes, the taa marboota (the mark of feminine word)
I declared my femininity a subject
And not an object

Poem 10

I sit on my bed complaining my loneliness
The sheets rebelled against my isolation
No one understands me except my pillow
Should I surrender to my bed's demands?
Or could I leave angrily and take my pillow?
The sheets are caught on fire with burning desire
My pillow reminded me that
These words are accompanied by tears and separation
The sheets demanded to overthrow my pillow
I wore a cloak of silence that doesn't fit me
And I became lonely missing my pillow

Poem 11

Read my poems
Learn my ideas
I am my own sponsor
I rule over my self and my life
I am not putting a cover on my head
And my body is not a receptacle
I liberated my body from shackles
I liberated my brain from stagnation
Enough rituals and announcing everyone is a non-believer
Did you cut my heart open and found the proof of non-believing?
Do you own the scale of good deeds?
Do you know the names of good Muslims?

O people of hypocrisy, I am Muslim in spite of the expert of Islamic jurisprudence
In the age of forgery I do not accept timidity

Poem 12
Moroccan national, with French demeanor and barbaric features
His love overwhelmed me as a wild horse
He fucked me, loved me, adored me
My lover's name is Abdel Wahed (Servant of the one)
I swear that he is the one
Come back to my bed for one day
Do you hear me Abdel Wahed?
I want one thing from you
I want the nectar of life
On my face, on my breast
Cover my animal desire with your juice
Receive my approval
And satisfy my desire

Poem 13
They call me a whore, debaucher, obscene woman
I am the sinner, I don't care about names
I am not a prostitute
Call me as you wish

Poem 14
I give you myself on my Sunna
Since everything I do is on my way
We don't need witnesses
You don't need promises
To my heaven lover you will inevitably return
Note:
Sunna is to follow the way of the prophet Mohamed's life.

Poem 15
I slept with men before you
Posers and charlatans

I swear that there is no man for me but you
In you I believe and on your love I depend
Note:
This verse could be viewed as blasphemous if interpreted as a
parody of Shihada (First pillar of Islam/testimony of faith)

Poem 16
The straight rod
I seek protection of my doomed devil
From a merciful God
I don't want my sins to be forgiven
I know that my words disgust you
Yes, I wear the veil
My face has repented
My body resists, refuses
And likes its torture
I seek protection of my doomed devil
From a merciful God
I do not want my sins to be forgiven
I walk on a straight path to hell
I do not feel alive
Unless I am on a straight rod
Note:
When you recite Koran, you start by saying I seek protection of
the merciful God from the doomed devil. There is a reference
in the first verse of Koran to people going to heaven being on
the straight path.

Poem 1

ياطائري العربي ،حلق في سماء رغبتي

أتحكم في هطول الأمطار

غزيرة،قليلة

قطرات ،قطرات

لمعاشرتي طقوس

ولعشقي ناموس

سأعلمك كل الرموز

أنا أقرر من يفوز

يا فرسي العربي

اركض في حلقة رغبتي

سريعاً،بطيئاً

توقف،توقف

أعطي لك التعليمات

أرسم لك الخطوات

هل عرفتني؟

أعرفك بنفسي:أنا التي تمتطي الجواد

Poem 2

في يوم الزفاف

كهدية للطهر والعفاف

قدمت لي أمي نصيحة

قالت لي كلمات صريحة

ضعفك هو قوتك

دموعك هي ذخيرتك

النساء كل النساء أمينة

وأمينة ترضي سيدها

كوني أنثى، كوني أمينة

كتبت دموع ذلها السطور

واستمعت في ذهول

بكيت انكسار أمي وميراثي النفسي

اعلنت استقلالي ورفضي لقدر غبي

Poem 3

الجنس صلاتي

تخلع نظراتك ردائي

تلهو هماستك بحياتي

تلمس رائحتك جسدي

تطهر قبلاتك صدري

تعبث اناملك بي

تحررني من قيودي

تغفر عني ذنوبي

تدخلني فتغمرني الحياة

Poem 4

اتيتك عارية من الكلمات

حبيبي, لا أجيد فن المناورات

عيوني لا ترسل اشارات

جسدي يبعث رسائل

فضها، اقرأها

ولا تقف امامي حائر

إضاعة وقتي من الكبائر

تريدني،اريدك

تشتهيني، اشتهيك

لا أهتم من بدأ

ولا يعنيني قول قائل

Poem 5

أدم حياتي تقبل اعتذاري

حبيبتي لا تتركيني

أخطات ازلني الشيطان

لا ازلنا الشيطان

سأرحل عنك

سأخرج معك

لا تترك النعيم

جنة ربي بدونك جحيم

ستعيش معي ملعون

سأبقى بدونك مجنون

أنا خائفة

حبنا هداية

والأرض؟

خروجنا بداية

Poem 6

يا قيس

احزن على فراقي ما حييت

اكتب في عيوني ما شئت

لم اكن ابحث عن قلب حنون

اردت معلماً لأنواع المجون

يا رجل ،عُرف عنك الجنون

وقابلتك بعيداً عن العيون

فوجدتك رجلاً من كلمات

وأنا يا حبيبي

لا أحب الشعر ولا الحكايات

اخترت رجلاً اخر

هو ليس بشاعر

لكن قلمه قلم قادر

هو لا يقرأ ولا يكتب

لكن سطر بداخلي ابيات

ابيات يُقص عنها روايات

Poem 7

قصيدة أم سرد

شعر أم خواطر

قوافي و قواعد

كلماتي نوع جديد

كلمات من دموع العبيد

لا أكتب قصيدة

كفانا قصائد

لا أكتب خاطرة

كفانا خواطر

كلماتي تمردت على البكاء

كلماتي رفضت الحياء

صديقي، لا تزن كلماتي

كلماتي تثقلها الأحزان

كلمات لا تقرأ

ولكن يشعر بها الابرياء

Poem 8

صار جسدي كبيت العنكبوت

وما ادراك ما بيت العنكبوت

اوهن البيوت لبيت العنكبوت

حلم يراودني

اراك واقعا بين الخيوط

اراك سعيدا تموت

قالوا راح فريسة

قلت راح شهيداً

حبيبته أنثى عنكبوت

Poem 9

ولدت أنثى

أسم مسبوق بحرف جر

أسم مجبور على الكسر

ولد رجل

أسم مبني على الرفع

أسم لا يعرف القهر

حللت كل تاء مربوطة

وأعلنت أنوثتي خبراً

خبر لا يجوز له إلا الرفع

Poem 10

اعتصم فراشي شاكيا وحدتي

تظاهرت الشراشف رفضاً لعزلتي

لا يفهمني إلا وسادتي

هل أخضع لمطالب فراشي؟

أم أرحل غضبا مع وسادتي؟

اشتعلت الشراشف رغبة واحتراق

ذكرتني وسادتي

هذة الكلمات يصحبها بكاء وفراق

طالبت الشراشف الإطاحة بدعامتي

أعلن فراشي قرار عزل وسادتي

ارتديت عباءة صمت لا تناسبني

وصرت وحيدة اشتاق إلى وسادتي

أقرأ اشعاري
تعلم افكاري
أنا ولية امري
أحكم في ذاتي وعمري
لن أضع على رأسي غطاء
وجسدي ليس بوعاء
حررت جسدي من القيود
حررت عقلي من الجمود
كفانا طقوس وشعائر
وكل من عليها كافر
هل شققت عن قلبي؟
ووجدت دليل كفري؟
هل تملك ميزان الحسنات؟
وتعرف اسماء الصالحات؟
يا أهل النفاق
أنا مسلمة رغم أنف الفقهاء
في عهد الزيف والرياء أنا لا أعترف بالحياء

Poem 12

مغربي الجنسية
فرنسي الطباع
بربري الملامح
اجتاحني حبه كفرس جامح
عاشرني، احبني ، عبدني
حبيبي اسمه عبد الواحد
وأقسم بأنه هو الواحد
عد إلى فراشي يوم واحد
هل تسمعني يا عبد الواحد؟
أريد منك شيئاً واحد
أريد سائل الحياة
على وجهي ،على صدري
غلف بسائلك شهوتي
تحصل على رضاي
وتشبع رغبتي

Poem 13

قالوا عاهرة، ماجنة، فاجرة
أنا الفاحشة ، لا تهمني الاسماء
لست داعرة تحترف البغاء
ادعوني كما تشاء

Poem 14

وهبتك نفسي على سنتي
فكل ما أفعله يا حبيبي على طريقتي
لا نحتاج لشهود
ولا تحتاج لوعود
لجنتي يا حبيبي حتما ستعود

Poem 15

عاشرت من قبلك رجال
ما بين مدعي ودجال
أقسم أن لا رجل لي إلا أنت
بك أمنت وعلى حبك توكلت

Poem 16

القضيب المستقيم
أعوذ بك شيطاني الرجيم
من رب رحيم
لا أريد لذنوبي مغفرة
أعرف كلماتي منفرة
نعم البس الحجاب
أقول لك وجهي قد تاب
لكن جسدي يأبى ، يرفض
يحب العذاب
أعوذ بك شيطاني الرجيم
من ربي الرحيم
لا أريد لذنوبي مغفرة
أنا على صراط الجحيم
لا أشعر بالحياة إلا وأنا على القضيب المستقيم

Made in the USA
Charleston, SC
01 November 2011